The information provided in this book is for informational purposes only and is not intended to be a source of advice or credit analysis with respect to the material presented. The information and/or documents contained in this book do not constitute legal or financial advice and should never be used without first consulting with a financial professional to determine what may be best for your individual needs.

The publisher and the author do not make any guarantee or other promise as to any results that may be obtained from using the content of this book. You should never make any investment decision without first consulting with your own financial advisor and conducting your own research and due diligence. To the maximum extent permitted by law, the publisher and the author disclaim any and all liability in the event any information, commentary, analysis, opinions, advice and/or recommendations contained in this book prove to be inaccurate, incomplete or unreliable, or result in any investment or other losses.

Content contained or made available through this book is not intended to and does not constitute legal advice or investment advice and no attorney-client relationship is formed. The publisher and the author are providing this book and its contents on an "as is" basis. Your use of the information in this book is at your own risk.

Copyright © 2024 by Jasbir Singh

All rights reserved.

No portion of this book may be reproduced in any form without written permission from the author, except as permitted by Canadian copyright law.

Bitcoin
A Catholic View

By Jasbir Singh

For my wife, Lea.

Contents

Preface 1
Chapter 1: Introduction 6
   Treasure 6
   A Taste of Money 7
   Searching for Something Better 11
Chapter 2: Financial Literacy 13
   The Money Supply 13
   Four Ways of Making Money 16
   Earn Your Own Keep 17
   Welfare 19
   Vocation 21
   Pokémon Cards and Economics 101 23
   Pizza and the Free Market 25
   Government Interference in the Free Market 28
   Property Rights and Free Speech 31
   Property and the Natural Law 33
Chapter 3: What is Money? 39
   Technology, Property, and Accounting 39
   The Physics of Value 41
   Power Projection 43
   History of the Ledger 45
   From Precious Metals to Paper 47
   Time Preferences and Cash 51
   Human Behaviour – Borrowing to Spend or Saving to Invest? ... 52
   Lesson from the Parable of the Talents 54
Chapter 4: The Technology of Bitcoin 57
   Trains and Blockchains 57
   Bitcoin Mining Details 60
   The Bitcoin Ledger 62

Chapter 5: The Value and Function of Bitcoin 65
   Value of Bitcoin 65
      Bitcoin is a Protocol 68
      Bitcoin is a Commodity 69
      Bitcoin is a Digital Asset 71
      Bitcoin is a Truth Machine 74
Chapter 6: Bitcoin is Unstoppable 77
   The State Versus Bitcoin 77
   Bitcoin's Competition 79
   Transition to Bitcoin Begins 82
   Failure of Keynesian Economics 84
Chapter 7: Morality of Money 88
   Is Money the Root of All Evil? 88
   Bitcoin is for Fairness 93
   Be Your Own Bank – Creative Disruption 95
   Bitcoin Mining is Green 98
   Burning Fossil Fuels is a Moral Imperative 101
Chapter 8: Why Invest in Bitcoin? 105
   Risk and Cryptocurrency Regulation 105
   Freedom and Time in the Future 108
   Fiat Money Erodes Time 112
   Widespread Bitcoin Adoption Coming Soon 115
   A New Paradigm with Bitcoin 118
Chapter 9: Two Sets of Ten Commandments 122
   An Open Heart and Mind 122
   The Ten Commandments 123
   The Ten Commandments for Financial Freedom 125
   Where Does Your Treasure Lie? 129
Acknowledgments 132
About the Author 133

Preface

Most of my family members and friends don't fully understand the importance of bitcoin. They are either indifferent to it, or they simply dismiss it outright as a scam or something to be avoided altogether due to the negative news that they may have heard in mainstream or social media. Some Muslim scholars also categorize bitcoin as *haram*, meaning forbidden or unlawful.

This negative sentiment towards cryptocurrency was researched in a recent academic study by Ashi Mann at Carleton University. The study involved a survey of cryptocurrency adopters and non-adopters about their experiences encountering cryptocurrency information or purchasing cryptocurrency. The results indicated that among non-adopters, feelings of fear, uncertainty, and doubt (FUD) originated from their general confusion about what cryptocurrencies are, how they operate, and their purpose. Non-adopters reported that reading news reports about scams and malicious cryptocurrency actors had deterred them from wanting to own cryptocurrencies[1].

It is understandable why many people are still skeptical of bitcoin. You cannot see it or touch it because it is not something physical. It exists in cyberspace as a digital asset, which may be difficult for most people to wrap their minds around. However, as a software engineer, I was able to comprehend the technology behind it, and why it stands out as a very significant invention in the field of computer science. It was only after understanding the technology behind bitcoin when I later realized it could function as money: a store of value and a medium of exchange.

It is true that some cryptocurrencies are scams, but bitcoin is not. Bitcoin is in a league of its own as the premier digital asset within the crypto industry[2]. After three years of my own research into bitcoin, I believe that it is the real deal. My hope is to convey the truth about bitcoin to you, and why I believe that it is on par with other revolutionary inventions, such as the wheel, the electric light bulb, penicillin, and the internet. I would even go as far as saying that people who truly understand bitcoin are *woke*.

Javier Milei, the newly elected president of Argentina, is an example of a woke politician. He believes that bitcoin is a solution to the problem of inflation. He stated: *"The point is that the first thing we have to understand is that the Central Bank is a scam. It is a mechanism by which politicians cheat the good people with the inflationary tax. What bitcoin is representing is the return of money to its original creator: the private sector."*[3]

Bitcoiners are woke because they can plainly see the injustice of the existing financial system with its poorly functioning government-issued currencies and the problem of inflation. Government-issued currencies have failed to preserve their purchasing power over time, and they do not serve as a good store of value. The current financial system favours the privileged minority and oppresses the majority. The rich get richer and the poor get poorer because inflation is built into the system.

The primary cause of inflation is government control over monetary policy. When governments and their central banks print and inject more money into the system, it causes inflation, which in turn has the effect of increasing the prices of assets. People who own assets, typically the wealthy, are rewarded by inflation because the prices of their assets increase over time, enabling them to preserve and increase their wealth. However, the majority of people who don't own assets, have to bear the burden of seeing the purchasing power of their money dwindle as their wages fail to keep up with the rate of inflation. The rising cost of goods and services makes it harder to pay the bills, let alone to save enough money to purchase a home.

Most of my friends are hard-working, middle-class husbands and fathers like me, who have been experiencing the pains of rampant inflation and the decreasing purchasing power of our money, especially during the aftermath of COVID-19 when governments around the world flooded the world economy with trillions of dollars. It has become a struggle to pay the bills and to make ends meet, especially for parents who are blessed with many children.

I believe that investing in bitcoin can help. Fortunately for us, as retail investors, there's an opportunity to purchase bitcoin before Wall Street and large financial institutions get involved, but time is running out.[4]

I felt a sense of urgency to write this book, not only to dispel the FUD surrounding cryptocurrencies, but to demystify bitcoin for my family, friends, and anyone else interested in discovering the true nature of bitcoin.

Bitcoin offers a way out of the existing financial system. It is an off ramp to a new financial order, which is better for the individual, regardless of a person's position or status in society. It can help people to save their hard-earned money in a way that preserves and even increases its purchasing power over time.

Bitcoin is turning out to be a lifeline for people who are suffering in countries with rampant hyperinflation. If bitcoin becomes a top world reserve currency one day, or if it becomes a financial settlement layer on which all government-issued currencies settle, then it will help over a billion people in the world without access to financial services, to begin saving and building a better life for themselves and for their families. Bitcoin is pro-life!

During my bitcoin journey, I developed a greater understanding and appreciation for what money truly is, and how it came into existence. At the same time I became more financially literate, and this inspired me, as a husband and father, to teach my wife and children about bitcoin and other important financial concepts. Public schools just don't teach financial literacy well enough.

For the benefit of parents reading this book, I have provided some explanations and examples about freedom, work, property, money and economics in a way that will hopefully help to educate the next generation. I also delve into the history and foundations of money, and how it arose naturally to facilitate trade.

My views on these topics are openly Catholic, and drawn from the wisdom contained in the New Testament of the Bible. I also draw inspiration from the moral teachings found in the Catechism of the Catholic Church, Catholic tradition, papal encyclicals, and from the writings of the saints. I discuss the morality of money and I also explain the technology behind bitcoin and how it works. At the end of the book, I share a set of Ten Commandments that I think can help anyone become financially literate with the hope of achieving financial freedom.

Today, money is issued into the economy by the State. This was even true at the time of Jesus as indicated in the passage below from the New Testament of the Bible:

> *"And they brought him a coin. And Jesus said to them, 'Whose likeness and inscription is this?' They said, 'Caesar's.' Then he said to them, 'Render therefore to Caesar the things that are Caesar's, and to God the things that are God's.' When they heard it, they marveled; and they left him and went away."*[5]

Imagine a world where the State no longer has control over money, and a new form of money arises from the private sector. This is what bitcoin is. It arose out of the private sector during the 2008 financial crisis, and it can only be influenced by free-market forces and the decisions made by free-thinking individuals. With bitcoin, there is no engraving of a person's head on it. There is no central government, no organization, nor committee that issues or controls bitcoin. Bitcoin has no owner, and it is truly decentralized money, operating by way of software code running on thousands of networked computers around the world. Bitcoin is true money of the people.

If Jesus came to us today rather than over 2000 years ago, then I suspect the updated version of what he said would be:

> *"And they showed him a bitcoin existing on the blockchain using their cell phone. And Jesus said to them, 'Whose bitcoin address is associated to this bitcoin?' They said, 'The owner of the private key.' Then he said to them, 'Render therefore to the rightful owner of the private key the things that are his, and to God the things that are God's.' When they heard it, they marveled; and they left him and went away."*

It is my contention that bitcoin may be the antidote to the problems that stem from our existing debt-based financial system. If bitcoin becomes a world reserve asset one day, then I believe it will have a positive impact on human behaviour, resulting in a reduction of violence, crime, and even war.

In the future, if more people prefer to hold bitcoin rather than their regular currency, governments will no longer be in a position to meddle with the economy through monetary policy. No government is capable of creating or controlling bitcoin. The impact of this may be profound, and I believe it will disable the State's ability to fund their war machine, the military industrial complex.

Chapter 1: Introduction

Treasure

When you were a child, did you ever dream about finding a lost treasure? I remember watching the 1981 movie, *Raiders of the Lost Ark*, and wanting to be like Indiana Jones who risked his life to find the Ark. My treasure-hunting romanticism faded away when I became an adult, but I still clung to the idea that I would find a treasure some day.

The first treasure in my life was discovered in 2002 when I attended a Catholic monastery in the province of Quebec. It was there that I witnessed the beauty and goodness of Christianity, and the Christian family life for the very first time. About a year after that experience, I converted to Catholicism, and Jesus would become the chief cornerstone of my life.

I found my second treasure in 2021, while painting my daughter's bedroom as I listened to a podcast about money and bitcoin. The promise of bitcoin opened my eyes to the ills of the traditional financial system, such as the problem of inflation and the devaluation of world currencies.

I think I was primed and ready to comprehend bitcoin due to my appreciation for the Christian moral value system, which recognized the dignity of the individual over the group. This was in contrast to the evils of Marxism, communism, and socialism (all rooted in collectivism), which valued the group over the individual. I discovered that not only could bitcoin function as a store of value and a medium of exchange, better than our existing government-controlled monetary system, but it could also function to reduce violence and war within and between nations. Fixing the money can fix the world[6].

Everything seemed relatively normal prior to COVID-19, but since then, many countries around the world discovered that they could not depend on each other for the exchange of goods and services as they used to. When the world came to a halt, it triggered a reaction that caused countries to become more self-reliant, and nationalistic. Resources are no longer being freely traded between nations and wars have sprung up, such as the war between Russia and the Ukraine, which revealed how imprudent it was for some European nations to depend on Russia for their oil and gas supplies. Global supply chains were severely impacted and prices sky-rocketed. Governments around the world reacted by flooding their economies with new money, which resulted in higher rates of inflation and even hyperinflation. More recently, Israel and Palestine (Hamas) are in open war with each other. Everything just seems all doom and gloom.

Enter bitcoin. Bitcoin is well positioned to bring relief to over 1 billion people who are excluded from the modern financial system. These people are either under banked or bankless. Fortunately, most people in the world have access to a cell phone, and those who do, are able to securely send, receive, and store bitcoin without fear of theft or confiscation from corrupt governments. The wealthy can now donate bitcoin directly to those in need, without the services of an intermediate third party. Bitcoin may be the most important earthly treasure of our time, yet to be fully understood and appreciated.

A Taste of Money

I grew up in a middle-class neighbourhood in Ottawa, Ontario, Canada. I had plenty of easy access to tennis and basketball courts, baseball diamonds, and football and soccer fields. By my late teens and early 20s, my time was mostly devoted to playing sports, having fun with my friends, and going to dance bars at night hoping to meet a pretty lady one day. I didn't think too deeply about other things, such as history, economics, finance, politics, or religion.

I just didn't want to grow up and become a responsible man, and I preferred to live a rather selfish and shallow lifestyle, remaining as a man-boy and avoiding responsibility as long as possible. I think I was influenced by the degrading culture of male immaturity as explained in a podcast interview[7] with Gary Cross, author of the book, *Men to Boys: The Making of Modern Immaturity*[8]. In the back of my mind, I knew that there was more to life than just playing sports and chasing after pretty women. One day, things would eventually have to change.

I am grateful to my parents for having instilled in me the value of getting a good education, and so I had already completed three undergraduate degrees in biotechnology, education, and software engineering by my early 30s. Also, thanks to my fiscally and socially conservative parents, I started paying more attention to politics and economics, and the opposing views held by the three major political parties in Canada: the Progress Conservative Party, the Liberal Party, and the New Democratic Party. I also began to learn about finance and investing from my father and elder brother, which made me appreciate the value of money.

At the time, I had no idea that money was continually being devalued due to inflation. It was the simple desire to have more money that motivated me to set out on a new track, one that offered hope for something better and possibly something more meaningful to focus on in life. It was time to start investing.

I never really gave much thought about money though, let alone investing, but I knew that it was better to have more money than less because of the basic utility of money. I just wanted more money to be able to buy life's essentials, and spend it on entertainment. It also made sense to save some money for a rainy day. I never once considered how money came into existence in the first place, its history, or how it is even defined. I don't think many people know what money really is until they take the time to properly study it.

I recall one particular evening in 1999, hanging out with my friend, Sumit, who had informed me about a new and upcoming high-tech company, called Research in Motion (RIM). The company had created a new wireless hand-held device, called the Blackberry, that could be used to surf the web and send emails. It had a monochrome screen and a trackball on the side of it. At the time, I had no idea how to evaluate companies or read company financial statements, but I didn't really care. I just believed in the product that RIM had produced, and as a *Star Trek*[9] fan, the thought of owning an electronic device that could connect to the web and send emails would make me feel like Captain Kirk or Commander Spock holding the infamous tricorder, while they explored new planets.

To this day, I recall the exciting moment when I made my very first online stock purchase by taking a gamble with $5000 to purchase 1000 shares of Research in Motion (RIM) stock at $5 per share. I logged into my personal computer, while Sumit was watching (he had never purchased a stock online either, so I was the guinea pig), and after a few mouse-clicks I had finally pulled the slot-machine lever to make the purchase. It was an incredible adrenaline rush.

The next day I went out to my nearest Rogers outlet, and I purchased the Blackberry RIM 957 hand-held device. I still own it to this day, as a souvenir and reminder of that day when my day trading experience began. For about a year, I used my Blackberry on a daily basis whenever I was out of the house to keep track of RIM's stock price and other stock ticker prices on the Toronto Stock Exchange.

After purchasing one thousand shares of RIM, a week or two later I decided to go all in and deploy an additional $10,000 of my savings (earned from my work in Japan) to day trade stocks as a hobby, which was really just a glorified form of gambling. I traded mostly high technology stocks on a daily basis from my bedroom, while living in my parents' house for a few months. I watched my $15,000 investment grow to $100,000 in those months, and my ego blasted through the roof. This was during the stock market dot-com bubble, and it was such a thrill to watch my money grow so quickly and easily.

My father always told me how hard it was to make money, and now I found myself questioning his wisdom since I had seen my investment grow with such little effort. Along the way, I also learned a few financial terms, such as price-to-earnings (P/E) ratio, market capitalization, and so forth.

But then within a few short months, the dot-com bubble burst in the infamous March 2000 stock market crash. I had lost all of my gains in a flash! The euphoria was over. What a shock and learning experience this was for me. I guess my father was right after all. I had learned my lesson the hard way, easy come easy go.

After this experience, I stopped day trading altogether, and I hung on to whatever cash that I had remaining. From then on, I would be a conservative investor, and take tips from my big brother about investing like Warren Buffet, a value investor, who, by the way, had avoided buying technology and internet stocks for the majority of his career, until he bought IBM in 2011, Apple in 2016, Amazon in 2019, and finally Google (Alphabet Inc.) and Shopify in 2022. Of course, it was a mistake to think like Warren Buffet, and I am still kicking myself for not purchasing 100 shares of Google stock at $85 per share in 2004 when I had the chance. I think my gut was still recovering from the roller-coaster ride of the dot-com boom and bust scenario just a few years prior.

Even though I continued to love technology, I knew that I had to stop gambling with my money, and I had to re-examine my life. I never really took money seriously in those days as my entire education was primarily focused on the life sciences and software engineering. I had intentionally avoided taking courses in economics, finance, or accounting because I thought those subjects were boring and relatively unimportant. That was a mistake that I would later come to regret. There I was, with a university education, but with no financial literacy apart from the bits and pieces I had picked up from my father and brother.

Searching for Something Better

After winning and losing money so easily as a day trader, my interest eventually turned towards religion. I was looking for purpose and meaning in my life, desperate and yet hopeful that there was something more to life than just eating, sleeping, having fun, and making money. Deep down I think I was yearning for some kind of true wisdom that no human or scientific study could provide, and I suspected that it could only come from the spiritual world.

After searching for happiness through earthly pleasures that would never satisfy me, no matter where I searched, I was always left with emptiness. Nothing could fill the hole inside of me. I experienced plenty of material comforts and pleasures, yet life just seemed pointless. I felt some kind of darkness within my spirit, and everything just seemed to be void of meaning and purpose. I think I was having an existential crisis, which triggered in me the search for God.

I began my search by studying multiple religions, looking for truth and wisdom. I couldn't find it in the eastern religions and philosophies. After becoming friends with a Catholic woman, she introduced me to a Catholic monastery where I learned about the theology and spirituality of Christianity directly from several monks. After visiting the monastery on multiple occasions, I was drawn to Catholic- tradition, spirituality, theology, and philosophy.

Later, I experienced what I think was a real miracle, my Jesus moment. It had a profound impact on me, and during that moment I dropped to my knees knowing that I wanted to be a disciple of Christ. I was baptized and confirmed as a Catholic in 2003, and I have been devoted to practicing my faith ever since. The story of my conversion can be found in, *Canadian Converts – The Path to Rome*[10].

My conversion opened my eyes to the beauty, truth and goodness of the Christian moral value system, which I came to realize was responsible for building Western civilization[11]. It also transformed my thinking from the secular left-wing liberal mindset on social and economic issues to a more mature and conservative mindset. I fully accepted Catholic moral and social teachings, which humbled and helped me to recognize that my ways were not God's ways. Somehow, becoming Catholic transformed me so profoundly that I believe it made me smarter and wiser compared to my previous self.

When I decided to learn about bitcoin in 2016, my mind was open, eager, and ready to study it fully without bias, just as I was open and willing to study Christianity. Studying bitcoin was not an easy task, but once I had completed my study, I became convinced about its tremendous value as a revolutionary technical invention having the power to modernize and transform the entire financial industry.

Chapter 2: Financial Literacy

The Money Supply

As I had no formal education in accounting or finance, it was bitcoin that triggered my interest and desire to become financially literate. Also, as a father, I felt responsible to educate my children about money, even though I had no basic understanding of the financial world, nor any idea how to properly manage my own money. This gap in my understanding was eventually filled in 2021 after reading the 1997 book, *Rich Dad Poor Dad*, by Robert T. Kiyosaki[12]. I wish I had come across this book twenty years ago, and I can't recommend it highly enough! It gave me the knowledge and confidence that I needed to speak to my own children about money.

After reading Kiyosaki's book, I started talking about money at the family dinner table. When my children asked me how I was able to obtain money in order to buy our house, car, and food for the family, I told them that I had to go to work every day, and that I got paid every two weeks. My children didn't know that I automatically received payments electronically directly into my bank account. I explained to them that I never actually saw the physical form of the money, but that I only made sure to check that the numerical amount of my pay was accurately recorded as a credit in my online account balance.

They also didn't realize that our local bank didn't really hold all of the physical cash in their bank vaults. At any given time, banks only hold 10% of the cash on hand, just in case customers wanted to make a cash withdrawal. If all customers were to suddenly show up at the bank to demand all of their money in cash, known as a bank run, then the bank would not be able to pay back all of its customers on that day. Bank runs are not common in developed countries, but they are common in developing countries when a currency suddenly collapses and becomes worthless due to hyperinflation. Recently in Lebanon, some of their citizens had resorted to robbing their own banks just to get their own money back! Lebanon's banks locked depositors out of their accounts because they just didn't have the money to cover bank withdrawals. This situation was fueled by Lebanon's hyperinflation crisis[13].

In their cute naivety, my children asked me ask why we couldn't just make our own coins or print our own dollars using our laser printer. I smiled and told them that, "Money doesn't grow on trees", and that if we tried to do that, it would be illegal, and we could go to jail for it. But actually I had to correct myself and inform them that money printing is exactly what the government does. When the government prints money and mints new coins, it is considered legal. But when someone else tries to do it, it is the crime of counterfeiting. I told them that governments around the world have been printing and controlling money for centuries, but that this could eventually change one day with the advent of bitcoin.

My children learned for the first time that bitcoin doesn't need a government to issue it. The State is no longer needed because the anonymous inventor of bitcoin, Satoshi Nakamoto[14], designed it in such a way that the bitcoin core software automatically issues bitcoins into existence, and records all peer-to-peer bitcoin transactions between people on an open and distributed accounting ledger without the need for a government-controlled central bank.

I also explained to them how traditional money flows through the existing financial system once created. In the case of the US, all monetary policy decisions are made by its central bank, the Federal Reserve, also known as the Fed. The Fed sets interest rates and creates new money. It directs the US Treasury to print dollar bills within the Bureau of Engraving and Printing. The United States Mint, also within the US Treasury, creates coins. The printed dollars and coins are then physically transported to commercial banks where people can obtain it.

The US Treasury issues government securities. These securities or treasuries exist in the form of treasury bonds, treasury bills and treasury notes. Treasuries are defined as *"... debt instruments in which investors are lending the U.S. government the purchase amount of the bond. In return, investors are paid interest or a rate of return. When the bond matures (or maturity date), investors are paid the face value of the bond."*[15]

The Fed increases the money supply by purchasing securities (usually Treasuries) in the open market. Banks can increase the money supply by lending money. The increase in the money supply is also known as increased liquidity, which means more cash is available to be spent by the people.

On March 26, 2020, the Fed eliminated reserve requirements in commercial banks. The reserve requirement is the amount of money that commercial banks keep on hand. By eliminating reserve requirements, banks no longer have to keep money stored within their bank vaults, thereby maximizing the money available to lend out to people. When banks increase lending to people, this increases the debt owed. All of this increased lending and debt creation occurs at the stroke of a keyboard.

The money eventually reaches the people when their bank account balances are credited after receiving a loan from a bank or receiving payment from an employer. In the case of a business or public sector institution, the employer has to pay its employees after employees have completed their work (proof-of-work system). Employees typically get paid every two weeks. In the case of a skilled trades person, such as a plumber or an electrician, they typically get paid after completing the job to their client's satisfaction.

Four Ways of Making Money

My children know that when they grow up, they can become anything they want. But I quickly realized that their idea about how to earn a living was very limited. I decided to show them Robert Kiyosaki's four basic ways to make money with some of my own examples. They could become an employee (E) like their father, a self-employed individual (S) like their uncle, who owns his own veterinary clinic, a business owner (B) like Elon Musk, or an investor (I) like Cathie Wood.

On a piece of paper, I sketched out four quadrants for E, B, S, and I (Figure 1), and I put it on our refrigerator door in the kitchen for my children to see. I explained to them that most people went to school first to get an education, and then after finishing school, they could find a job and go to work as an employee, or they could be self-employed if they were really good at selling a service or product to others. Every now and then over a few weeks, I would point to the refrigerator door and ask them: "What do you want to be when you grow up, an E, S, B, or I?"

I encouraged them to think beyond being an E, and to become a B, S, or I. To become a business owner, they could start out working as an employee for a while, but they should think about using their savings to start and build their own business, or try to become self-employed. If they had enough money, they could also purchase an existing business, such as a Domino's Pizza franchise. Having a business is a very good thing because it is foundational to how wealth is created by offering goods and services that people desire, and it provides jobs to people who are looking for work.

If they had any extra money left over, they could invest it by purchasing assets. I explained to them that an asset was anything valuable that they could own, such as gold, real estate, shares of a company - stocks, or digital assets such as bitcoin. Some people are really good at investing, and they can literally watch the value of their assets increase over time. The extra money could be put to work for them, instead of working to make money.

I suggested that if they really wanted to become financially wealthy, it would be better to be self-employed, a business owner, or an investor, rather than an employee. I also told them that it would be wiser not to save their money in a bank, but to use the money to purchase an asset as an investment.

An important lesson I took from Robert Kiyosaki is that poor people save and spend their money, but rich people use their money to invest and buy assets. These assets could then be sold later at a profit to continue buying even more assets.

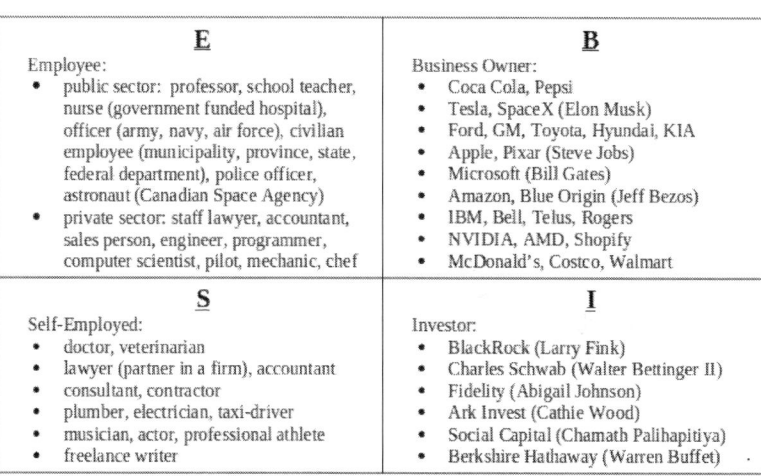

Figure 1 – The four ways to make money, adapted from Robert Kiyosaki's book, Rich Dad Poor Dad

Earn Your Own Keep

People can be lazy sometimes, and some of us are tempted to take the easy way out by acquiring things for nothing without working for it. An attempt to correct this way of thinking was made over 2000 years ago in St. Paul's letter to the Thessalonians. He advised that the right thing to do is to work to earn a living, rather than being idle and dependent on others. He stated: *"If anyone will not work, let him not eat."*[16]

Walter E. Williams (1936-2020), distinguished American Professor of Economics at George Mason University, linked work to money. He described money as being a certificate of performance, which could be used to purchase 3 pounds of steak and a six-pack of beer:

> *"Suppose you hire me to mow your lawn and afterwards you pay me $30. The money you pay me might be thought of as a certificate of performance – proof that I served you. With these certificates of performance (money) in hand, I go to my grocer and demand 3 pounds of steak and a six-pack of beer that my fellow man produced. In effect, the grocer says, 'Williams, you're asking that your fellow man, as ranchers and brewers, serve you. What did you do in turn to serve your fellow man?' I say, 'I mowed my fellow man's lawn.' The grocer says, 'Prove it!' That's when I hand over my certificates of performance – the $30."*[17]

Williams also defined social justice as being the right to keep your own hard-earned money. He said that it is only fair to keep what you earn, and that we should not concern ourselves with what others earn because it belongs to them. Any kind of social justice, which forcibly takes money from one person to give to another would be considered immoral. I agree with his definition of social justice:

> *"But let me offer you my definition of social justice: I keep what I earn and you keep what you earn. Do you disagree? Well then tell me how much of what I earn belongs to you – and why?"* -- Walter E. Williams

A similar lesson is provided in the famous *Parable of the Workers in the Vineyard* from the Gospel of Matthew. Some of the workers argued with their employer because some of them had to work longer hours than others for the same pay. There were grumblings about the workers who worked very few hours. The employer replied to them saying that each employee agreed to their hours of work and pay, and that it was the employer's right to pay whatever was agreed upon. This statement by the employer is a good lesson, which I shared with my children:

> *"...Friend, I am doing you no wrong; did you not agree with me for a denarius? Take what belongs to you, and go; I choose to give to this last as I give to you. Am I not allowed to do what I choose with what belongs to me? Or do you begrudge my generosity?"*[18]

However, the deeper meaning behind this parable is that God gives out his mercy to all of his children as he so pleases, regardless of our own effort. How God rewards others should be of no consequence to us, and so we should not compare ourselves to others. For example, the thief on the cross, who repented of his sins, received the same reward of eternal life as Jesus' devoted disciples. In other words, everyone has hope if they have truly repented of their sins, even right down to the last second.

Welfare

Welfare is a government program that exists in many countries to provide financial aid to people who can't work. It is meant to be a safety net for people who become unemployed, and who truly can't work for short periods of time. This may happen in times of illness or a job loss.

However, some people abuse the welfare system by collecting welfare cheques from the government even when they are capable of working. This is called welfare fraud. People who commit welfare fraud are basically cheating the system by staying idle rather than going to work. If a society has too many people on welfare, it can be a problem because the hard working people would resent having to pay taxes to support the welfare program.

Some people think that the State should not create a welfare system because the government is known to be wasteful, inefficient, and in most cases, abusive of its powers. People who share this view argue that if the government creates large and expensive welfare systems, then society will effectively become a nanny State.

A nanny State is over protective of its citizens, and can even become intrusive to the point of interfering with how people choose to freely live their own lives. For example, the State can impose rules, barriers to purchase, and higher taxes on consumable products, such as cigarettes, cannabis (marijuana), and alcohol under the guise that the government is protecting the health of its citizens.

This means that the government can decide what is appropriate and what is not appropriate, thereby robbing citizens of their rights and freedoms. Thomas Sowell, another very distinguished economist, disagrees with the nanny State, and shares a similar view with Walter E. Williams. He questions the idea of greed, and makes a very good point:

> *"I have never understood why it is greed to want to keep the money you have earned but not greed to want to take somebody else's money."*

Another way to help the unemployed, without becoming a nanny State, could be to let the private sector take care of the poor and less fortunate among us through private charities. A private charity is also capable of identifying people who may need financial assistance, and it could be more efficient and less of a burden on tax payers. This is a debate about whether the public sector or private sector should take care of the unemployed.

Vocation

In teaching my children about their Catholic faith, I shared the following quote from the Old Testament, which explains why we have to work in order to live. God basically commanded us to work, and on top of that, he humbled us by letting us know that we are dust, and to dust we shall return:

> *"… cursed is the ground because of you; in toil you shall eat of it all the days of your life; thorns and thistles it shall bring forth to you; and you shall eat the plants of the field. In the sweat of your face you shall eat bread till you return to the ground, for out of it you were taken; you are dust, and to dust you shall return."*-- Book of Genesis 3:17-19

Catholics believe that God has a purpose and mission for everyone. This mission is referred to as a vocation, which is God's invitation to live a life according to his unique plan for each of us as individuals.

There are typically four vocations, or calls to holiness, that a Catholic can choose to live their life by: as a celibate single person; as a married person; as a priest; or as a religious person living as a monk or a nun in a monastery or convent.

I explained to my children that God loves them on a personal level, and that when they become adults, they should try their best to discern what they think God's plan is for them. I shared this quote with them so that they could appreciate their own worth in God's eyes:

> *"Before I formed you in the womb, I chose you; before you came forth from the mother's womb, I consecrated you."*[19]

My children know that they are free to choose whatever vocation aligns with their life's meaning and purpose. Even though society imposes expectations such as climbing the corporate ladder as high as possible, I told them that they didn't have to meet anyone's expectations other than their own self-imposed ones.

For example, they could lead full and meaningful lives even by devoting themselves to work for a non-profit organization or a charity to help the less fortunate among us. There are many charitable organizations, such as Chalice and World Vision, which sponsor children around the world to help them with food, water, medicine, shelter, clothing, and education. For example, some Catholics have chosen to live off of the donations of others, which is common for monks or nuns in a monastery or convent.

For men who wish to become a priest, the work typically involves taking care of the sacramental and spiritual needs of the people in a local parish. Priests are busy people, administering the holy sacraments at weddings, baptisms, and confirmations, and celebrating Mass during weekdays and on weekends. They also hear confessions, visit hospitals to anoint the sick, and officiate at funerals. On top of all of this, they provide spiritual and pastoral care to the Catholic laity (ordinary members of the Catholic Church).

I made sure to let my children know that God loves them unconditionally and in a personal way. All that he asks of us is to love him back, and to love our neighbour as ourself. No matter what work we choose to do, it should always be done in a way that is worthy and pleasing to God, and which helps to build a loving, healthy, and civilized society that respects the sovereignty of the individual and the rule of law. The two commandments that Jesus gave us summarizes it completely:

> *"Teacher, which is the great commandment in the law? And he said to him, "You shall love the Lord your God with all your heart, and with all your soul, and with all your mind.*

> *This is the great and first commandment. And a second is like it, You shall love your neighbour as yourself. On these two commandments depend all the law and the prophets."*[20]

I try to inspire my children to be the best version of themselves, which includes doing their school work and chores as best they can, not for their parents or for their teachers, and not even for themselves – but for the glory of God. Saint Josemaría Escrivá, Spanish Roman Catholic priest and founder of Opus Dei, captured the essence of this idea about work being an offering to God, by stating the following important lesson about work:

> *"It is no good offering to God something that is less perfect than our poor human limitations permit. The work that we offer must be without blemish and it must be done as carefully as possible, even in its smallest details, for God will not accept shoddy workmanship. 'Thou shalt not offer anything that is faulty,' Holy Scripture warns us, 'because it would not be worthy of him.' For that reason, the work of each one of us, the activities that take up our time and energy, must be an offering worthy of our Creator. It must be operatio Dei, a work of God that is done for God: in short, a task that is complete and faultless."*[21]

Pokémon Cards and Economics 101

When we work, we expect to receive money in return for our labour. But why does money have any value at all? I remember asking my daughter, when she was ten years old, what she thought was her most valuable possession. At the time, she responded that it was her Pokémon card collection. She instinctively knew that some of her specialty Pokémon cards were more valuable than the others because they were rare and desirable.

I explained to her that when something is rare, it is scarce.

Scarcity occurs when there isn't enough of something to satisfy everyone, or if there is a high demand for something that is in short supply. This leads to the definition of economics. *Economics is the study of human action under scarcity* (Saifedean Ammous).

She could easily understand that her Pokémon cards had value because many children her age, even adults, liked to play the game and collect the cards. Value can therefore be defined as the utility or desirability something has, which is recognized as being worth possessing. According to Saifedean Ammous, value is a subjective valuation by an individual. He provides the following definition of value: *"Value is our subjective assessment of the satisfaction we derive or expect from goods and services."*[22]

When enough people recognize the utility or desirability of something through their own individual value judgment, then the marketplace determines the price of an item, which fluctuates with the forces of supply and demand.

Prices are expressed in the particular currency depending on where you happen to live in the world. I explained to my daughter that where we live in Canada, the currency is called the Canadian dollar, and so when we see price tags at the store, the items are priced in Canadian dollars. In the US, the currency is called the US dollar. In the United Kingdom, it is the Pound sterling, and in Mexico, it is the Mexcian peso. To know the approximate value of something, we typically rely on the price to give us a signal about the object's worth, but in the end it comes down to each person's individual subjective valuation.

To explain how the forces of supply and demand worked, I explained that if something is scarce and desirable, then it will likely have a higher price tag. When something is plentiful or abundant such as bottled water, then it will have a lower price tag. The air we breathe is everywhere in plentiful supply, and so it is free! If suddenly, the maker of Pokémon cards decided to print a lot more of my daughter's favourite specialty cards, then the supply would go up, making it more plentiful, and therefore the price would drop. It made sense to her that if there is an abundance of something, and it is easy to get, then it should have a lower price tag.

There is often a desire to hold scarce assets for a long time, and she understood the concept that an asset's value could increase in the future based on the forces of supply and demand. I suggested that she should take care of her Pokémon cards, and keep them in mint condition. She agreed.

So, the price of an item should fluctuate over time, depending on the forces of supply and demand in the free market, but quite often the prices of assets just keep rising for no apparent reason. One such reason is inflation, which I would explain to her another day. This discussion about my daughter's Pokémon cards helped her to understand the basic principles of economics. I wish I had understood this when I was a child at her age!

The price tag of an item is only a signal of its value, and this is only true if the currency is stable and retains its value over time. Unfortunately, in countries with high inflation or hyperinflation, the currency is unable to retain its purchasing power. This results in price signals being grossly distorted, making it difficult to determine the appropriate value of a product or a service. Nonetheless, possessing assets is critical to being able to preserve wealth. My daughter knows that her Pokémon cards are worth more than the Venezuelan bolivar!

Pizza and the Free Market

It is natural for a society to rely on the forces of supply and demand to determine the prices of goods and services within an economy. When this happens naturally, without government interference, then this is said to be a well-functioning free market. Countries that have a free market are typically wealthier than those countries that don't.

In countries where the State controls the prices of goods, the people are typically poorer and don't have access to high-quality goods and services. America, for example, has a free market economy, which is common in democracies. But for some countries, such as Venezuela and Cuba, which are not democratic, they have poorly functioning markets. The natural forces of supply and demand are disrupted in these countries, and the people struggle to buy what they need to have a good life. Poverty is common in these countries where prices of goods and services are artificially set by the government. People can't get what they need, and sometimes they have to stand in long lines just to buy the basic necessities. Even then, supplies usually run out.

In Canada, which has a reasonably functioning free market, most people can buy everything that they need to have a comfortable life. For example, when I order pizza for a family supper, I have a variety of pizzerias to choose from. Each pizzeria has a slightly difference taste, and they all have slightly difference prices. When I shop for pizza, I take a mental note of the prices, and I like to order from the pizzeria that I think has the best price for the quality that I know my family prefers. If one of the pizzerias is more expensive than the other, without the quality or taste being that much different, I probably wouldn't order from that pizzeria. This means that the owners of the pizzerias have to check to see if their prices are competitive. I explained to my children that the owners probably visited each others' pizzerias in the neighbourhood to compare menus and prices in order to help them decide how to set their own pizza prices.

When the owners of pizzerias can freely adjust or modify the prices of their pizzas at any time, this is a very good thing. Countries that have well-functioning free markets, without interference from the government, allow private business owners to set their own prices for the products and services they are selling, and they can hire employees at whatever hourly wage is agreed upon. This exemplifies the parable of the workers in the vineyard, where the owner of the vineyard pays the labourers whatever agreement has been made voluntarily.[23]

The owners of pizzerias in Ontario, Canada, however, are not quite so free to pay their chefs and pizza delivery drivers whatever wage they wish. The Ontario government has enforced a minimum wage of $16.55/hour as of October 1, 2023. This has a negative impact on all small business owners such as a pizzeria. At the end of each business day, if a pizzeria doesn't earn more money selling pizzas than the cost of paying employee wages and other expenses, such as pizza ingredients, pizza ovens, rent, and utilities, then the pizzeria might not earn enough profit to stay in business. The government's interference in forcing business owners to pay a minimum wage of $16.55/hour may result in having to fire some employees to reduce expenses, or potentially cause the pizzeria to shut down its business altogether.

When pizzeria owners have the freedom to set their own prices and employee wages, then they have a better chance of staying in business. However, if the government interferes, this will disrupt the free-market system from working optimally. In this way, minimum-wage laws do more harm than good because it makes it harder for small businesses to operate, and it makes it harder for them to hire staff.

For people looking for work at a pizzeria, it would be better to get hired and earn a wage than not to be hired at all. The negative impacts of minimum-wage laws is very well explained by Henry Hazlitt in Chapter 19 of his 1946 book, *Economics in One Lesson*[24], where he states the harm caused by government enforcement of a minimum wage within an economy:

> *"You merely deprive him of the right to earn the amount that his abilities and situation would permit him to earn, while you deprive the community even of the moderate*

services that he is capable of rendering. In brief, for a low wage you substitute unemployment. You do harm all around, with no comparable compensation."[25]

Government Interference in the Free Market

When a government imposes minimum-wage laws or interferes with the operations of a business, then businesses are more likely to fail or not even get started in the first place. Entrepreneurs may become demotivated when governments over-regulate their businesses. This often occurs in socialist and communist countries. By forcing entrepreneurs to set their prices or wages according to government rules and regulations, it takes away their freedom and motivation to run their businesses as they see fit. Imagine if the government went so far as fixing the prices for all pizzas sold in a pizzeria? Does that sound fair to the pizzeria owner?

In some socialist and communist countries, where the government interferes with businesses and over regulates them, the natural forces of supply and demand fail to operate. Socialism and communism are immoral because the system of government controls and regulations are severe, which results in poorly functioning businesses and fewer jobs. If companies fail, then more people become unemployed. When this happens, the people not only become poorer compared to other countries that have a free market, but they are also deprived of the goods and services that the businesses could have offered. When a business is discouraged to start up in the first place, which is often the case in socialist and communist countries, this also results in less variety. Imagine if there was only one pizzeria business operating in an entire city!

In a nutshell, socialism and communism are immoral because the government takes away the freedom of business owners to run their businesses as they see fit. When businesses are not allowed to set their own prices for the products and services they sell, or to set employee wages at a level they think is best for their business, then they are likely to fail in making a profit. The idea of making a profit is anathema to socialists and communists. However, for people living in free-market economies, profit is a powerful and necessary incentive to drive innovation for the production of goods and services that customers need and want. Henry Hazlitt contrasts the private sector and the State by saying: *"The 'private sector' of the economy is, in fact, the voluntary sector; and ... the 'public sector' is, in fact, the coercive sector."*[26]

Socialism and communism have been complete failures in society, resulting in a death count of over 100 million people in the 20th century alone. The Nazi Party in Germany, founded as the National Socialist German Workers' Party, and its socialist orientation towards supporting the working class, exterminated 6 million Jews. In the Soviet Union, under Joseph Stalin, the death count of his communist regime is estimated to be 20 million or higher. In communist China, the death toll is estimated to be 65 million as a result of Mao Zedong's attempt to create a new socialist China through the extermination of his number 1 enemy, the intellectual. In communist Cambodia, the Khmer Rouge under the leadership of Pol Pot, systematically killed 1.5 to 3 million citizens.

The Catholic Church strongly opposes collectivism. *Article 1* on *The Person and Society* from the *Catechism of the Catholic Church*, discusses the principle of subsidiarity, i.e., a recognition that the good of the individual person is primary in any organization or community:

> *"The principle of subsidiarity is opposed to all forms of collectivism. It sets limits for state intervention. It aims at harmonizing the relationships between individuals and societies ..."*[27]

29

Article 7 on *Economic Activity and Social Justice* from *The Catholic Catechism of the Catholic Church* declares that the principle task of the State is to guarantee *"individual freedom and private property, as well as a stable currency and efficient public services."* Unfortunately the State has failed in most of these tasks. *Article 7* also comments on the responsibilities of business enterprises, which are to *"consider the good of persons and not only the increase of profits ... profits are necessary ... they make possible the investments that ensure the future of a business and they guarantee employment."*[28]

Javier Milei, the president of Argentina, recently addressed the World Economic Forum in Davos. In his speech he stated that the Western world is in danger of moving towards collectivism and socialism, the root cause of poverty.[29]

The opposite of collectivism is individualism. In a free-market economy, every individual matters, and every individual has the right to life, liberty, and to own private property. The best depiction of the virtues of individualism and self-interest over collectivism can be found in the books, *The Fountainhead*[30] (1943) and *Atlas Shrugged*[31] (1957) by Ayn Rand. I don't agree with Rand's views on sexual morality as portrayed in these two books, but she clearly exposes how government intervention can destroy the human spirit, creativity, and productivity. These two books are timeless, and they should be required reading for all young adults, in my opinion.

One of the best scenes from *Atlas Shrugged* is *the money speech* delivered by the character, Francisco d'Anconia. He rejects the notion that money is the root of all evil, and instead he sees money as the root of all good. He describes money as a tool to facilitate trade and human relationships. Money is the result of wealth created by men, and this wealth comes from individual ideas translated into voluntary effort and productivity. When material goods are produced, this gives rise to money in order to be able to *"... deal by trade and give value for value"*. An excerpt from the scene is provided below:

> *"'So you think that money is the root of all evil?' said Francisco d'Anconia. 'Have you ever asked what is the root of money?' Money is a tool of exchange, which can't exist unless there are goods produced and men able to produce them.*
>
> *Money is the material shape of the principle that men who wish to deal with one another must deal by trade and give value for value. Money is not the tool of the moochers, who claim your product by tears, or of the looters, who take it from you by force...Until and unless you discover that money is the root of all good, you ask for your own destruction. When money ceases to be the tool by which men deal with one another, then men become the tools of men. Blood, whips, and guns – or dollars. Take your choice – there is no other – and your time is running out."*

Property Rights and Free Speech

Because money is owned by people, the concept of property is fundamental to understanding money and assets. My children instinctively thought that property was equivalent to land, but this is not correct. I explained to them that property is not really the land, but rather it is the ownership relationship between a person and the land or any object for that matter. If land or an object is possessed or owned by a person or an organization, then that object can be said to be property. If there happens to be a plot of land somewhere that is not owned by anyone, then it would not be considered property. My daughter now understands that her Pokémon cards are her property, only belonging to her and nobody else.

Property can be categorized as being either public or private. Public property is owned by the State, and it is dedicated for public use, whereas private property is owned by an individual or company. Understanding property as ownership sets up the idea of property rights. If somebody takes your property without your consent, then that would be stealing. If someone uses your property without your consent, that would be trespassing.

Apart from the obvious human rights such as the right to life, liberty, and freedom of religion, the right to own property is also a fundamental right. In fact, the right to own property impacts the right to free speech. For example, people are free to speak their mind on public property (in the case of democratic countries), but people are not free so speak their mind on private property. If someone speaks offensively to the property owner while trespassing, then the owner has the right to tell the person to get off their property for any reason, even if they don't like what they are saying. There are laws that permit the forcible removal of a trespasser if necessary using lawful means.

In the public square, freedom of speech is a right in democratic countries, and listeners do not have the right to not be offended. Free and democratic societies allow free speech even if it is offensive to others. A clear example of an infringement of free speech occurred in 2016 at the University of Toronto, a public research university, when Professor Jordan Peterson, and all professors, were compelled by the university to use gender-neutral pronouns preferred by students.

Jordan Peterson rightly objected to using specific language that was imposed upon him by the State[32]. This is entirely different from banning specific offensive words on the grounds of hate speech, which is fair and just, but in Jordan Peterson's case, the State was compelling him to use specific language that the students insisted that he use. There are simply no grounds to compel people to use specific words when speaking, and this is based on the history of English Common Law. Jordan Peterson was correct and courageous to stand up for his right to free speech.

Property and the Natural Law

Rights, such as the right to life, liberty, and the right to own property come from the Natural Law, which posits that there exists a God-given and self-evident universal moral order that humans can comprehend naturally.

Natural law theories were first documented in ancient Greek and Roman philosophy, separate from Judeo-Christian philosophy. Both Aristotle and Cicero spoke of a universal or natural law, which is in accordance with nature. Cicero wrote that natural laws were eternal and immutable for all time, commanding us to do what is right, and forbidding us to do what is wrong. For Cicero, the natural law obliges us to contribute to the general good of the larger society, thus promoting virtue.

There are also references to a natural or moral law in the Old and New Testaments of the Bible[33]. In the Book of Hebrews from the Old Testament, there is a reference to God's placement of his laws into the minds and hearts of his people:

> *"This is the covenant that I will make with the house of Israel after those days, says the Lord: I will put my laws into their minds, and write them on their hearts, and I will be their God, and they shall be my people."*[34]

In Saint Paul's Letter to the Romans from the New Testament, he refers to the law written on our hearts:

> *"Therefore you have no excuse, O man, whoever you are, when you judge another; for in passing judgment upon him you condemn yourself, because you, the judge, are doing the very same things...They show that what the law requires is written on their hearts, while their conscience also bears*

> *witness and their conflicting thoughts accuse or perhaps excuse them on that day when, according to my gospel, God judges the secrets of men by Christ Jesus."*[35]

The Natural Law was further developed in the Middle Ages by Christian philosophers, such as Albert the Great and Saint Thomas Aquinas. According to Saint Thomas Aquinas, the Natural Law is one of four laws.

The first of these laws is the Eternal Law, which comes from the Divine wisdom of God, and it is not fully knowable by humans. The Eternal Law describes how people ought to behave. Everything in nature reflects the Eternal Law, which is universal and unchanging.

Second, there is the Divine Law, which St. Augustine described as being guided beyond the world to eternal happiness in the City of God. These laws originate from revelation, which were revealed in the sacred scriptures of the Old and New Testament. These laws provide guidance on right behaviour and exercising judgment. For example, the 10 Commandments that God gave to Moses are an example of the Divine Law.

Third, is the Natural Law, where private and public property rights come from. The English philosopher, John Locke, believed that the Natural Law promoted life, liberty, and the right to own property. The Natural Law is the foundation for legal traditions today. We recognize these laws from our own human reason, and they form a certain moral compass within us, which God placed into nature, and therefore into us. All people have inherent rights, not given to us by legislation, but by God, nature, or reason. Unfortunately, communist countries don't recognize the right to own private property, and this deviates from the Natural Law.

The *Catechism of the Catholic Church* defines the Natural Law as follows[36]:

> *"The natural law expresses the original moral sense which enables man to discern by reason the good and the evil, the*

truth and the lie:

> *The natural law is written and engraved in the soul of each and every man, because it is human reason ordaining him to do good and forbidding him to sin ... But this command of human reason would not have the force of law if it were not the voice and interpreter of a higher reason to which our spirit and our freedom must be submitted.*
>
> *The natural law is nothing other than the light of understanding placed in us by God; through it we know what we must do and what we must avoid. God has given this light or law at the creation.*
>
> *The natural law, present in the heart of each man and established by reason, is universal in its precepts and its authority extends to all men. It expresses the dignity of the person and determines the basis for his fundamental rights and duties:*
>
> *For there is a true law: right reason. It is in conformity with nature, is diffused among all men, and is immutable and eternal; its orders summon to duty; its prohibitions turn away from offense .... To replace it with a contrary law is a sacrilege; failure to apply even one of its provisions is forbidden; no one can abrogate it entirely.*
>
> *The precepts of natural law are not perceived by everyone clearly and immediately. In the present situation sinful man needs grace and revelation so moral and religious truths may be known 'by everyone with facility, with firm certainty and with no admixture of error.' The natural law provides revealed law and grace with a foundation prepared by God and in accordance with the work of the Spirit."*

One can use reasoning to deduce what is good and preferable according to the Natural Law. In Table 1 below, I have provided a sample of contrasting words to convey the understanding of beauty, truth, and goodness in the left column contrasted with the opposite meaning in the right column.

Beauty – Truth - Goodness	Opposite
moral, good, virtue	immoral, evil, sin, vice
love, joy	hate, pain
true, truth	false, lie
humility, meek, modesty	pride, arrogant, narcissism
trustworthy, fair, just	dishonesty, foul, corrupt
beauty, grace, clean	ugliness, inelegance, stained
free, freedom, liberty, sovereignty	slave, servitude, serfdom, oppression
peace, harmony, order, straight	violence, chaos, disorder, deviation
live, life, save	murder, abortion, euthanasia, suicide
wise	foolish
generous, give	covet, crave, steal
reveal, expose, uncover	deceive, cheat, misinform
temperate	harsh, uncontrolled
prudent, careful	reckless, careless
healthy	sick
chastity, celibacy, virginity	fornication, promiscuity, impurity
monogamous	polygamous
marriage	separation, divorce
individualism	collectivism
capitalism	Marxism, socialism, communism, fascism
democracy	autocracy, tyranny
competition	monopoly, cartel, oligopoly

Table 1: A sample of contrasting words, which can be known from the Natural Law

If I were to add bitcoin to Table 1, it would be added to the left column. To be discussed later in Chapter 5, bitcoin is considered to be a *truth machine*, which makes it fit nicely on the left-hand side. All other government-issued fiat currencies should be placed in the right column because they are susceptible to manipulation in their supply, thus impacting inflation.

Finally, there are lower-level human laws, which we see all around us, such as street traffic signs, and other kinds of rules to maintain law and order within a society. These human laws help to create a safe and civilized society. Driving faster than the speed limit when driving will break our human laws, but it would not break God's Eternal Law, the Divine Law, or the Natural Law. Saint Thomas Aquinas concluded that human laws should conform as closely as possible to the Natural Law to be considered legitimate.

This understanding of the Natural Law and property rights provided me with an opportunity to discuss it with my children. I explained to them how their mother's grandparents were negatively impacted in Czechoslovakia during communism. Under the Communist Party of the former Soviet Union, the government confiscated private property from the Czech people, stripping away their private property rights altogether. This meant that citizens could no longer own private property.

In my wife's case, the government seized her grandparents' apartment building, which according to the Natural Law, is equivalent to stealing. People don't often think of the government stealing from its own citizens, but this is exactly what communist regimes often do. Conditions were so terrible under communism, that people had to stand in long lines to purchase the basic necessities of life. My wife recalls having to wait in long lines to purchase bananas, and she was taught to scrape and eat the insides of banana peels so as to not waste any of it.

Fortunately, my wife and her parents escaped from communist

Czechoslovakia in 1986, and they restarted their new lives as refugees in Canada. Through hard work and determination, they were able to eventually purchase their own home, free from the tyranny of communism.

The good news is that Czechoslovakia returned to democracy and freedom in 1989 (Velvet Revolution) with the fall of the Berlin Wall. The new democratic government was able to return some of the private property back to their original owners.

Chapter 3: What is Money?

Technology, Property, and Accounting

Learning about the Natural Law made me think more deeply about money and how it originally came into existence. As indicated in the previous chapter, money can be thought of as a certificate of performance, to prove that you did some work when serving your fellow man. Therefore, money is a proof-of-work technology that can be used for trading with others to purchase goods and services.

When you earn money, it should be yours to keep, and nobody else should be allowed to take it away from you forcibly. Having freedom means to be able to transact with others on a voluntary basis. This is in keeping with the Natural Law. Because money can be owned, money is property. Property rights exist to protect owners.

Today's government-issued currency is typically secured with the help of a 3rd party custodian such as a bank. Most of us store our money in a bank, but this has its problems. It enables the State to take our money from us forcibly through taxation or government order if it wishes. For example, French economist, Frederic Bastiat, argues that taxation is legal plunder[37], and American economist, Murray Rothbard, argues that taxation is theft[38].

Today, the State has the power to freeze anyone's bank account or garnish the wages of those who fail to pay their taxes. The government is also capable of taking money from law-abiding citizens through slow and subtle means such as money printing, which is a direct cause of inflation and devaluation of currency.

We intuitively expect money to hold its value and purchasing power over time, but this is not the case. All traditional currencies used today depreciate in value over time due to inflation. How much value a currency holds depends on a country's strength in the world and its use of monetary policy. Monetary policy is a mechanism by which central banks manipulate the money supply and interest rates. It is well known that the US dollar is currently the strongest currency in the world. For example, 1 US dollar (USD $1) is worth more than 1 Canadian dollar (CAD $1).

Money is typically used as a medium of exchange, a store of value, and a unit of account. When the State creates and issues money, the money begins at the central bank and then it flows to commercial banks where it eventually reaches the people.

Every time something is bought or sold, it is called a transaction. Transactions are recorded by the banks when the money flows from one business or individual to another. After money is first printed at a central bank or created electronically with a few key-strokes on a computer, it then flows through the financial system to other banks, businesses, and eventually to the people.

The banking system has a way of crediting, debiting, and reconciling the various accounting ledgers, which are maintained by the banks. The system of accounting ledgers is based on double-entry accounting, which was invented and published in 1494 by the Catholic Franciscan Friar monk and mathematician, Luca Paciola (1447-1517), who is considered to be the father of accounting and book-keeping. His accounting system was soon adopted by the famous Medici banking family of Florence, Italy.

The Physics of Value

Getting to the root of the meaning of money requires some knowledge of physics. Real-world physical concepts, such as energy, work, and power can help in understanding the utility of money as a store of value and a medium of exchange.

Energy is typically stored in the earth in chemical form, such as oil, or geothermal energy such as the heat from volcanoes. Energy is also stored within light from the sun, and leaves can transform this light energy from the sun into food through the process of photosynthesis.

Work is defined as the energy transfer that occurs when energy is expended to achieve something. In physics, work is typically defined as the energy expended to move an object over a distance. Energy and work are measured in Joules, named after the English physicist, James Prescott Joule.

If energy is expended, but the object doesn't move, then no work is accomplished.

Mathematically, 1 Joule is equivalent to the energy expended when applying a force of 1 Newton (N) on an object with a mass of 1 kilogram (kg) to move it a distance of 1 metre (m). Expressed as an equation, this becomes:

work = Force x distance, or

J = N x m, where 1 N is defined as the force applied on a mass of 1 kg causing it to accelerate at a rate of 1 metre per second, per second.

Since $N = kg \cdot m/s^2$, therefore Force = mass x acceleration, which is Newton's 2nd law of motion.

Figure 2 – 1 Joule of work is accomplished by moving a 1kg object a distance of 1 metre

Work can be done quickly or slowly, and so the time (in seconds) that it takes to accomplish work is defined as power. Power is the rate at which work gets done, measured in Watts (W). Expressed as an equation, this becomes:

Power = work / time, or
$W = J / s$

The above mathematical equations simply demonstrate the physical reality of energy, work, and power, which can be thought of as being captured by money. Because money can be thought of as a certificate of performance for doing work, this means that it represents proof that energy was expended to accomplish the work.

This is the fundamental reason why money possesses value. Using this understanding, if a lot of energy is expended to do a lot of work over time, then a large amount of money would be needed to capture this energy, work, and power. This implies that when we do work, we should get paid proportionately to the work accomplished.

When someone possesses money, this sends a signal to others that energy was expended to do work. Viewed in this way, money can be thought of as a store of energy, work, and power accomplished. This is the reason why people can use money to purchase goods and services provided by others.

Once people recognize an object as possessing value in the way just described, then it will become desirable to own, and people will be willing to trade with it as a medium of exchange, i.e., a currency. Understanding the physical reality of energy, work, and power explains why money has value, and why it has manifested itself in printed notes and metal coins.

Power Projection

It's hard to imagine living without money today, and without the double-entry accounting system developed by Paciola over 500 years ago, but humans did live without money in pre-historic times during the Paleolithic and Mesolithic stone ages. When humans hunted for food and lived in hunter-gatherer societies, there was no need for money.

Homesteading may be the closest approximation we have to living a life style of self-sufficiency. Imagine growing your own wheat to make your own bread, or killing a pig to make your own pork chops! That's a lot of work to do on a daily basis, just to eat and survive. Doing all of this work alone is not efficient, and eventually society evolved to producing greater efficiency gains through specialization and cooperation (bartering).

A hunter has to be able to acquire enough energy from food to be able to transform it into the kinetic energy of doing the physically demanding work of hunting. When food is consumed and converted to energy, some of this energy is converted into kinetic energy for the purpose of stalking and chasing after prey, and creating weapons to be able to do the hard work of trapping and killing an animal.

Before the existence of money, people invented and used tools to make hunting and gathering more efficient. Hunting, therefore, is really about power: the use of energy to do the maximum amount of work in the shortest amount of time. Those civilizations that could maximize their power through the use of better tools and technology advanced more quickly.

Humans soon realized that they could use power to fend off attacks and secure more resources. In fact, the entire food chain is linked to the idea of work optimization to achieve physical security. From unicellular organisms to humans, life is about the securing of resources in the environment, such as territory, food, and water to be able to support life and to flourish.

Those civilizations that could best optimize power to secure their property and resources, and use power to impose a physical cost to an attacker, were better able to survive and flourish. Those civilizations that could not optimize power well enough, did not flourish.

The concept of power optimization, known as power projection, is not only applicable in the physical world, but it also applies in cyberspace. Bitcoin has recently been recognized as the best technology in existence that can be used to protect a nation's interests within cyberspace.

Bitcoin uses energy to produce work and power using the most cryptographically secure computer network in the world. For this reason, bitcoin has been described as a power projection phenomenon in the book, *Softwar: A Novel Theory on Power Projection and the National Strategic Significance of Bitcoin*, by Major Jason Lowery.[39] Lowery believes that bitcoin is critical for the US military's national security. The following is an excerpt taken from his thesis:

> *"Bitcoin could represent the dawn of an entirely new form of military-grade, electro-cyber information security capability – a protocol that people and nations could utilize to raise cyber forces and defend their freedom of action in, from, and through cyberspace. The bottom line is that Bitcoin could represent a softwar or electro-cyber defense protocol, not merely a peer-to-peer electronic cash system."*

Therefore, bitcoin could change the future of national strategic security and international power dynamics in ways that we have yet to understand. We know how significant power projection was from the discovery of the atomic bomb, which ended World War II. A civilization with the best power projection capability usually advances their own interests the most, and is able to secure the most resources, and win wars.

History of the Ledger

When hunter and gatherer societies were able to develop their power projection tools to become more efficient at gathering food and protecting their resources, they eventually began to accumulate a surplus of goods, which enabled them to barter and trade with each other. This enabled more advanced societies to flourish, i.e., pastoral societies, horticultural societies, and agrarian societies[40].

Each barter or transaction was eventually recorded to keep track of the ownership of the items being traded, their quantity, the date, and the parties involved. Before the existence of paper, transactions were recorded on a ledger (a record keeping system) made from various kinds of materials. For example, the ancient Sumerians of Mesopotamia (3500-3000 BCE) used clay tablets known as *proto-cuneiform*, which were laid out in rows and columns, to keep track of trades. The ledger of transactions showed details such as the amount of grains, fish, pots, and tools that were traded, and on what date, with a signature to show that it was certified and authentic. These ledgers were maintained to manage the transactions in a community, and it helped to settle disputes.

People eventually realized that trading pots and pans for food wasn't very effective or efficient, and they soon decided to use some kind of token, such as shells, glass beads[41], or precious metals representing an equivalent value of the item being traded. Tokens were much easier to carry and to exchange exact amounts of value.

The tokens themselves were a kind of validation or proof that an equivalent amount of work was done in some capacity to provide value in society. If the work was done to physically mine or acquire a precious metal out of the ground, and people were willing to accept it as money, then the token entered circulation as a medium of exchange for the purpose of trade.

According to biblical accounts over 3000 years ago, King Solomon and the Queen of Sheba possessed gold and silver. From that time onward, the Hebrews used silver shekels as the unit of measure.

During the time of Jesus around 2000 years ago, Judas Iscariot, the betrayer, was paid 30 shekels of silver to betray Jesus as recorded in the New Testament:

> *"Then one of the twelve, who was called Judas Iscariot, went to the chief priests and said, 'What will you give me if I deliver him to you?' And they paid him thirty pieces of silver. And from that moment he sought an opportunity to betray him."*[42]
>
> *"When Judas, his betrayer, saw that he was condemned, he repented and brought back the thirty pieces of silver to the chief priests and the elders, saying, 'I have sinned in betraying innocent blood.'"*[43]

Today's transactions are stored on accounting ledgers recorded on centralized computers and servers maintained by commercial banks. We trust these banks as intermediate 3rd party systems to maintain accurate records of our transaction histories. Money is credited (money in) or debited (money out) from our bank accounts. Those of us who are fortunate enough to even have access to banking services are able to log into our own online bank account to view and validate all of our transaction histories.

Rather than using a centralized system of computers and servers, bitcoin now enables a distributed and decentralized accounting ledger that can record all individual peer-to-peer bitcoin transactions, without needing any 3rd party system. This distributed ledger is known as the blockchain.

Bitcoin perfectly stores all peer-to-peer transactions on thousands of computers around the world (more details about this later). Banks are no longer necessary to manage transactions, and as more and more people become aware of this technology, it will be more preferable to use because of its superior security and transaction integrity (more details about this later). Bitcoin may one day transform or even replace the entire banking industry. The Medici era of banking could be on the verge of extinction!

From Precious Metals to Paper

Precious metals such as gold and silver were used as a medium of exchange and a store of value in centuries past. They are both durable, but they are too heavy, and they are not easily transportable. They are somewhat divisible, but not that easily. Gold coins were too heavy to transport in large quantities, and so it became easier to just store the gold in a warehouse, and then issue a paper certificate representing a claim to the equivalent amount of gold held in storage. People could then use these paper certificates to make purchases, and then the new holders of the certificates could return to the warehouse to redeem their gold. This is where the expression, "as good as gold", comes from.

Relying on people to be the custodians of gold within a warehouse became problematic. Some custodians of gold started cheating by issuing more certificates than the amount of gold stored in the warehouse. Eventually, people possessing gold certificates caught on to this scam when they returned to the warehouse to redeem their gold, only to discover that there wasn't enough gold in the warehouse to honour their certificates. The custodians were caught committing fraud by issuing counterfeit gold certificates.

The United States government also got into the business of being the custodian of gold by establishing Fort Knox (1935) as the country's main gold reserve backing the US dollar. The citizens of America and people in other nation states trusted the US government to protect their gold as they knew that the gold was needed to back the US dollar. However, trusting the government became problematic after winning World War II when the US government started printing more US dollars than the amount of gold held at Fort Knox. In other words, the US government was effectively committing the crime of counterfeiting, but doing so was considered legal because the government was doing it.

When other countries started to make requests to redeem their gold from Fort Knox, similar to a bank run, the United States had no choice but to officially end the gold standard, which President Nixon declared in 1971. Since then, the US dollar has become a floating currency without any backing by a precious metal.

The reality is that government-issued currencies today are worth no more than the paper they are printed on. Some people even argue that today's currencies are really backed by the military power of the nation, and that the monetary system itself has become a power projection game[44]. The US government, for example, has been abusing its ability to print as much money as it wishes, by decree (fiat), to fund whatever project or military cause it wants to fund.

The financial term used to express money printing or increasing the money supply within the economy is called, Quantitative Easing (QE). When the money supply grows more rapidly than the economic output of a country, then inflation occurs. *"During COVID-19, the Federal Reserve materially increased the nation's money supply. As a result, the nation experienced higher-than-usual inflation."*[45]

Inflation also results in a decrease of purchasing power, also known as the debasement of a currency. For example, the US dollar has suffered debasement to the point where $1 in 1971 is now equivalent to $7.10 today.

Inflation becomes noticeable when you compare prices over time. For example, in 1967, you could buy a BigMac hamburger from McDonald's for $0.25, but today that same hamburger costs $4.00. Nothing about the BigMac hamburger has changed, but the price has increased due to the effects of inflation. When the government keeps increasing the money supply, it causes the prices of goods and services to increase. Unfortunately, wages don't keep up with inflation, and so purchasing power continues to decrease.

Money can only retain its value if it is scarce. But if money grew on trees, which it literally does in the case of government-issued currency, then its over supply will continue to cause inflation and a reduction in the purchasing power of money. This is precisely the phenomenon being observed today.

According to a graph published by the Federal Reserve Bank of St. Louis (Figure 3), the United States of America took drastic measures during COVID-19 by quintupling (5X) the money supply from USD $4 trillion in 2020 to USD $20 trillion by December 2021[46].

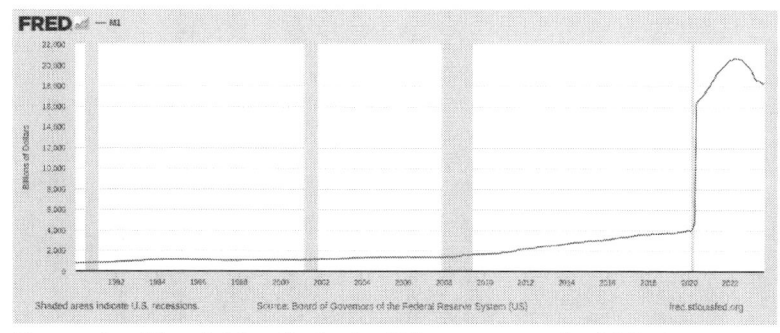

Figure 3 – Five-fold spike in the US money supply (M1) since COVID-19 from 2020 to December 2021.

Governments often decide to increase the money supply because they think that it can stimulate the economy, a principle from Keynesian economics, but what truly ends up happening is that the increase in the money supply causes inflation. This inflation causes prices of goods and services to increase, while reducing purchasing power. Everyone becomes poorer every time the Fed decides to increase the money supply. It is crazy to think that only a few people in America have this power to manipulate the money supply. Regardless of good intentions, the Fed has increased the money supply too quickly, causing inflation, and increasing poverty.

Inflation is one reason why homelessness continues to increase. Lack of affordable housing means that more people are priced out of the housing market as single income earners. More often than not, two incomes are needed to purchase a house. This wasn't the case a few decades ago when single income earners could afford a home. In the 1970s, my father was able to purchase the proverbial single family home with a white picket fence, while my mother was a stay-at-home mom. Because of inflation, this is no longer possible for the majority of people. Inflation has debased the purchasing power of money so much that living standards and affordability continue to fall. Keynesian economics has clearly failed in this regard.

Time Preferences and Cash

In the 1960s, there was a famous *Marshmallow Test*[47] by Walter Mischel, which has become well known for the rewards of foregoing instant gratification. In the study, children were presented with two options: they could either immediately take one marshmallow presented before them, or they could wait fifteen minutes knowing that that they would receive two marshmallows.

The study found that the children who caved into instant gratification by taking the one marshmallow were not as successful as the children who were able to wait fifteen minutes for two marshmallows. In other words, delaying instant gratification, with the hope for more in the future, proved to be a predictor of success later in life.

Another way of restating the concept of avoiding instant gratification is to say that it is better to have a lower time preference. Time preference is the value one places on receiving a good or service at an earlier date compared to receiving it at a later date. Having a high time preference means choosing to have instant gratification rather than waiting. In general, a person who is able to lower their time preference by delaying instant gratification, is more able to build a better future.

Today, when people earn money, they can choose to spend it immediately, or they can save it for something better in the future. Giving up or delaying what you could have right now only works if the money being saved can retain its value over time. Those who save for something better in the future depend on money holding its value. This is a very important concept because it helps to understand the concept of investing in assets as opposed to saving cash.

According to billionaire investor, Ray Dalio, "cash is trash"[48] because it loses its value over time. Converting spare cash to an asset is better because assets generally retain their value or increase in value over time, with the hope of outpacing inflation.

Human Behaviour – Borrowing to Spend or Saving to Invest?

People instinctively know that saving money can help them to make a more expensive purchase in the future. In this way, it delays the purchase if you don't have enough money at the present moment.

When I asked my children what they would do if they didn't have enough money to buy a used car when they turned 18, they said that they would have to wait until they saved enough money. This is certainly one way to make a large purchase, but what if they really needed the car to get to school or to work, and there was no public transportation in the area? How would they be able to buy a used car?

They said that they could borrow the money from a bank, and then pay the bank back later. When I asked them why the bank would agree to lend thousands of dollars to a student to buy a car, they didn't know, and so began another discussion about how banks operate, and what's in it for the banks.

When a commercial bank gives out a bank loan to a person or a business, the bank doesn't have to worry about having enough money because they know that the central bank can just digitally provide the bank with more money as it needs it. For this reason, commercial banks aren't too concerned about loaning out money.

Bank loans create a debt, and this debt is equivalent to increasing the money supply. Today's society is largely built on debt rather than savings. It's no wonder why almost anyone can purchase a $40,000 car without actually having $40,000 cash on hand. People in North America literally don't own their cars and homes because they are using borrowed money from a bank (debt) to purchase them. They agree to pay back the loan with interest over several years of monthly payments.

This understanding about debt and interest would become the next lesson for my children. I explained to them that if they wanted to buy a car in the future, they could try to borrow the money from a bank. For example, the bank might agree to loan them $12,000, but they would have to pay back the loan with interest and other fees in monthly payments over a period of typically 5 years (60 months). If the bank charges 5% interest, then these monthly payments would be approximately: $12000 / 60 months + interest/fees per month = $226.45 per month. This would translate to a total payment of $226.45 x 60 months = $13587. That's an extra $1587 in interest paid to the bank to borrow $12,000 up front to purchase the car.

I reminded them that they would also need to purchase auto insurance, which might cost an additional $150 per month. My children intuitively knew that it wasn't a good deal to pay that amount of interest, especially when compared to a lower interest rate such as 1% or 2%. I think I was able to convince them that it would be better to use public transit rather than buying a car because it would be more affordable for them.

I then tried to convince them that they could use their extra savings to buy assets instead of a car. I showed them how to spend $5000 of virtual money to simulate the purchase of stocks using the portfolio tracking features of Yahoo Finance. I encouraged them to think about their favourite companies, and to look at price charts over the last few years. Using the same chart on the refrigerator door (Figure 1), which showed examples of public companies that sold shares on stock exchanges, I asked them to figure out how many shares of certain companies they could purchase with their $5000. After inputting the data into Yahoo Finance together, we compared everyone's portfolio to see who was winning over time. It became a fun game.

It has been gratifying for me as a father to be able to teach my children about investing in assets, such as Pokémon cards, coins, or company shares. They now know that it is better to use cash to purchase assets, which have the potential to increase in value over time, rather than spending their money to obtain immediate pleasure and instant gratification. I showed how assets tend to appreciate in value, and how they could even be worth millions of dollars in the future.

When I showed them examples of what some old Pokémon cards and coins were worth today, they were shocked. It was a real eye-opener for them. I told them how much I had regretted not saving my old hockey cards of Wayne Gretzky. My own children now have a chance to purchase assets with the expectation of reaching a higher value over time. This helped them to understand the concept of investing. Unfortunately, I have not yet been able to convince them that bitcoin is the best asset around. That's why I needed to write this book.

Lesson from the Parable of the Talents

The idea of investing existed even in Biblical times. There is a lesson from the *Parable of the Talents*[49] in the New Testament, which teaches that God expects us to increase the value of the gifts and talents that are given to us.

Even though God has no use for money, and we can't work our way to Heaven through our own efforts alone, God does expect us to use the gifts that he has given us to do good in the world, even if that means taking risks.

The good that we can do involves serving our fellow man in a way that expresses our love and care for one another. I explained to my children that they should strive to make a contribution to the world in the form of goodness, truth, and beauty, which could help them discover the meaning and purpose of their lives.

Also, it is clear from *The Parable of the Talents*, that investing and taking risks is a responsibility. We just need to be careful not to idolize anything above God, and to avoid the trap of loving money or objects for the thing itself. It is good to want to make a lot of money for the purpose of doing good in the world, in a selfless rather than a selfish manner.

The *Parable of the Talents* states how important it is to be like the first two servants rather than the third servant. The first two servants were faithful, and they both pleased their master because they invested their talents and were able to return more than they were given. The third servant; however, was lazy and fearful, and chose to do nothing with his talent, other than burying it in the ground. This excerpt of the *Parable of the Talents* was taken from the New Testament of the Bible:

> *"For it will be as when a man going on a journey called his servants and entrusted to them his property; to one he gave five talents,to another two, to another one, to each according to his ability. Then he went away. He who had received the five talents went at once and traded with them; and he made five talents more. So also, he who had the two talents made two talents more. But he who had received the one talent went and dug in the ground and hid his master's money.*
>
> *Now after a long time the master of those servants came and settled accounts with them. And he who had received the five talents came forward, bringing five talents more, saying, 'Master, you delivered to me five talents; here I have made five talents more.' His master said to him, 'Well done, good and faithful servant; you have been faithful over a little, I will set you over much; enter into the joy of your master.'*
>
> *And he also who had the two talents came forward, saying, 'Master, you delivered to me two talents; here I have made*

two talents more.' His master said to him, 'Well done, good and faithful servant; you have been faithful over a little, I will set you over much; enter into the joy of your master.'

He also who had received the one talent came forward, saying, 'Master, I knew you to be a hard man, reaping where you did not sow, and gathering where you did not winnow; so I was afraid, and I went and hid your talent in the ground. Here you have what is yours.' But his master answered him, 'You wicked and slothful servant! You knew that I reap where I have not sowed, and gather where I have not winnowed? Then you ought to have invested my money with the bankers, and at my coming I should have received what was my own with interest.

So take the talent from him, and give it to him who has the ten talents. For to every one who has will more be given, and he will have abundance; but from him who has not, even what he has will be taken away. And cast the worthless servant into the outer darkness; there men will weep and gnash their teeth.'" -- Matthew 25:14-30

Thinking more deeply about this parable, another interpretation is that it is not the case that the third servant who received one talent and buried it was punished by an angry God. Rather, it is meant to show that we should not cling to ourselves and to our possessions[50]. The message for us is to be generous with what we have, to take risks, and to promote the flourishing of others. Investing was a concept that Jesus addressed over 2000 years ago, in favour of putting money (talents) towards ventures that had potential to reap rewards and higher returns. In other words, being productive and increasing wealth is a very good thing when that wealth is used to glorify God and help others.

Chapter 4: The Technology of Bitcoin

Trains and Blockchains

In 2010, I heard about bitcoin for the very first time. I also learned that people could mine bitcoin using their own computer, but I instantly thought it was some kind of worthless video-game token or fake coin used for online gambling. I completely rejected it based on my uninformed and biased view. When I heard about the 2014 crash of the infamous cryptocurrency exchange, Mt. Gox[51], it only confirmed my view that bitcoin was a scam.

However, in 2016, I heard about blockchain technology, and I became very intrigued and excited about it. My interest in the technology behind bitcoin made me consider purchasing bitcoin at that time. But again, I did not purchase it because I was put off by the hassle of having to create a cryptocurrency wallet, which I did not completely trust. The technology just didn't seem ready.

A few years later in 2019, I learned about another huge scam in Canada when cryptocurrency holders lost approximately $130 million from the fallout of the Canadian cryptocurrency exchange, QuadrigaCX. This particular cryptocurrency exchange had no oversight, and it was not regulated by a securities commission. The Chief Executive Officer of QuadrigaCX, Gerald Cotten, was discovered to have misused client assets for years, unchecked and undetected, for his own personal enrichment. His company collapsed in early 2019 following his death in 2018.

But around the same time, after reading Satoshi Nakamoto's foundational 2008 *Bitcoin White Paper*[52], I was able to recognize and appreciate how elegant and powerful blockchain[53] technology truly was. I think my background as a software engineer really helped me to understand the paper. For the very first time, a completely decentralized and open network became available to anyone for the purpose of securely sending and receiving digital money in a peer-to-peer manner without the need for the services of a trusted third party. It was a trustless system that worked because of cryptography.

Most people think that anything digital on a computer can be copied as many times as desired, and this is certainly true for documents, images, audio files, etc., but with bitcoin it is impossible to make copies of it because bitcoin transactions are stored with a unique cryptographic signature known as a hash, making the blockchain immutable and censorship resistant. I recognized the use of cryptography as being fundamental to digital money if it were to work.

So what is a blockchain? One way to understand it is to visualize a train system comprised of train tracks, train stations, and individual passenger cars making up a single train on the track. During train operations, a trainman is needed to link cars together with train couplings. A train conductor is needed to validate passengers' train tickets when boarding, and a train engineer operates the train. Each train station has a copy of the map of the entire train system. Train stations can communicate with each other to ensure that they all possess the latest information about the passengers on the train. At each train station, the passenger's tickets can be checked by train conductors to ensure that there are no stowaway passengers riding for free.

Keeping this train analogy in mind can help to understand the blockchain with the following terms:
- internet – the network infrastructure that allows information to travel through network wires and cables between servers and to personal devices, analogous to the network of train tracks and train stations in a train system
- nodes – the computers connected to the internet, where

each node runs a copy of the bitcoin core software, and records all bitcoin transactions entering the network, analogous to the train stations where passengers board, and where train conductors and train engineers work
- block – a data structure storing approximately 2000 to 4000 bitcoin transactions, where each block has a storage capacity of 1 megabyte, analogous to a passenger car holding passengers
- cryptography link – a unique digital fingerprint (technically known as a hash) that scrambles the contents of each block so that they can be linked together to produce the blockchain, analogous to a train coupling used to link passenger cars together
- bitcoin miner – the owner of a specialized node, who runs the necessary computer hardware devices (application-specific integrated circuits), which are needed to generate enough computing power to do the work of validating transactions and adding new blocks to the blockchain with the cryptography link, analogous to a trainman who does the work of operating train couplings to physically link the passenger cars together

A blockchain then, is comprised of individual blocks, where each block stores bitcoin transactions. Think of each bitcoin transaction as a passenger on the train. Just as the train conductor has to do some work to validate everyone's ticket, a bitcoin node has to check and verify each bitcoin transaction by propagating it across a network of thousands of nodes to ensure every node is synchronized. The bitcoin miners then accomplish the work of adding a new block to the chain by expending enough computing power to generate the correct cryptographic hash when generating each new block's unique signature hash.

All nodes are synchronized in 10-minute intervals every time a new block is added, and each block contains an identical copy of the blockchain ledger of transactions. This redundancy of the ledger makes it resistant to bad actors. Bitcoin is said to be censorship resistant because of the high energy and computing power that goes into doing the work of strengthening the network's security. The high energy and computing power makes it cost prohibitive for bad actors to successfully attack it.

The bitcoin core software issues new bitcoins as a reward to the bitcoin miner who successfully adds a new block to the blockchain. In the case of a train, the train conductor doesn't get paid for every car that gets filled with passengers, and the trainmen don't get paid for every train car that gets linked to a car using a train coupling, but on a blockchain, a bitcoin miner gets rewarded with bitcoin after successfully adding a new block.

In this way, the bitcoin core software replaces the need for a government or central bank to print new money into the economy. This is the fundamental reason why bitcoin is a revolutionary invention. The bitcoin core software is flawless and produces a perfect ledger, unlike humans operating a bank, who are prone to temptations, errors, and misjudgments.

Bitcoin Mining Details

Bitcoin miners need to compete with each other if they want to earn new bitcoin rewards. This competition involves an incentive mechanism known as proof-of-work. The proof-of-work mechanism requires bitcoin miners to invest in equipment and resources (electricity and computing power) to enable them to validate all of the transactions in a bitcoin block before successfully adding the block to the blockchain. Miners have to purchase expensive computer hardware (mining rigs) with application-specific integrated circuits that can generate enough computational power to successfully mine blocks.

These days, miners are no longer home-garage setups. Mining

has evolved to using industrial-strength data centres or large scaled bitcoin-mining farms, to do the work of (1) searching for a random number using sheer brute force, (2) combining that number with the transactional data in a bitcoin block, and (3) hashing all of that data using the SHA-256 cryptographic algorithm to successfully link a new block to the blockchain.

SHA-256 is a one-way cryptographic hashing function, invented by the United States government's National Security Agency in 2001. SHA stands for Secure Hashing Algorithm. Hashing is analogous to making a scrambled egg. Once the egg has been cracked, scrambled and cooked on a frying pan, it is impossible to return back to the original unbroken egg.

The SHA-256 hashing function executes the process of accepting any digital input, such as a word, phrase, novel, photo, audio file, or video file, and then it transforms it into a scrambled output of fixed length characters. The output, also referred to as a hash, is an alphanumeric string of characters representing the digital signature of the original input data. For example, the hash of *hello world* is the alphanumeric string of characters, a948904f2f0f479b8f8197694b30184b0d2ed, and it is impossible to go backwards to determine the original input.

To this day, over twenty years later, the SHA-256 algorithm has never been decoded or compromised. It has proven itself to be tamper-proof, making it impossible to derive the original input given the output hash.

So, a miner will be successful at mining a bitcoin block if the hash value they produce starts with a specific number of leading zeros (the number of zeros changes, acting as a difficulty adjustment factor). As more computational power is used to speed up the hashing process, the bitcoin core software automatically adjusts the mining difficulty level to maintain a constant 10-minute block-creation time, which is why the blockchain was originally thought of as a time chain[54].

It takes a lot of energy and computational power to produce the correct hash, which is like finding a needle in a haystack. The incentive for a miner to pay for electricity, and invest in expensive machinery to do the work, is a reward of 6.25 newly minted bitcoins (BTC) plus the bitcoin transaction fees. If the price of 1 BTC is US$40,000 (as it was at the time of this writing), then this would equate to a reward of US$250,000 per block.

The bitcoin reward is halved every four years, known as the *halving*, which is written into the software code. In the next four-year cycle, beginning in April 2024, the bitcoin reward will be halved to 3.125 bitcoins per block. When this happens, miners' revenues will be halved, which means lower profits, and possibly even a loss. If miners experience a loss, then it won't be worth their while to continue mining, unless they are able to reduce their expenses or if the price of bitcoin increases in the marketplace. The price of bitcoin has historically increased after every bitcoin *halving*.

The Bitcoin Ledger

Think about all of the data that exists within each passenger car of a train and all passenger cars combined. Every passenger's name and the amount paid for a train ticket was recorded by the train conductors when the passengers boarded. For every passenger car of the train, there is a permanent record, and this record, or ledger, can never be altered.

Now imagine that anyone in the world can view this ledger by using an online web browser. This means that the ledger is open and transparent for public viewing. This is the case for the bitcoin blockchain. Although it is open and transparent for public viewing, it does not record any names of individuals. The bitcoin core software only records an individual's bitcoin public address. This preserves the anonymity of individuals on the blockchain. Each bitcoin public address appears as a long alphanumeric string of characters between 26 and 35 characters in length, and they all begin with either a "1", "3", or "bc1".

The bitcoin ledger contains all of the bitcoin transactions for every block, and only the bitcoin public addresses and the amounts sent and received are visible to the public. For example, the very first bitcoin address (The Genesis Address) was recorded as: *1A1zP1eP5QGefi2DMPTfTL5SLmv7DivfNa*.

This address can still be found in the first block, known as the Genesis Block, and it was created and released onto the internet by Satoshi Nakamoto on January 3rd, 2009. There are now over 800,000 blocks making up the bitcoin blockchain network, storing the full history of all bitcoin transactions ever made. Imagine a train with over 800,000 passenger cars, which continues to add a new passenger car filled with passengers every 10 minutes. All of this information makes up the bitcoin ledger.

But where does this ledger actually reside? Imagine every train track being the network links making up the internet, and every train station functioning as a node. If every train station has a copy of all of the data in every train car running on the track, then every node has a copy of the entire bitcoin ledger of transactions.

There may be hundreds of train stations in a country. With bitcoin, the exact number of nodes making up the network is difficult to know, but some have estimated it to be well over 15,000[55]. Every single node runs the same copy of the bitcoin core software, and each stores a copy of the blockchain, which is the ledger itself.

The advantage of having thousands of copies of the ledger distributed across all 15,000 nodes is that it makes it next to impossible to modify the ledger. The network is resistant to hackers, system failures, and power outages, and if any problems occur at one node, then all of the other nodes will automatically detect the problem and drop the node.

The method used to accomplish this feat is known as bitcoin's proof-of-work consensus mechanism whereby all of the nodes agree on the transaction data stored in the blockchain. This consensus mechanism incentivizes the miner nodes to behave ethically, thereby securing the network and giving each miner a chance to successfully validate the next block. If they don't behave ethically, then they lose their chance of earning the bitcoin reward[56].

So what does all of this mean? Basically, the invention of the bitcoin blockchain has made it so that the two parties who want to send and receive bitcoin to each other can do so in a secured peer-to-peer manner for the very first time. They don't have to know each other, and they don't have to trust each other. Since trust is no longer required, it is called a trustless network.

The bitcoin core software automatically processes the transactions, thereby eliminating the need to have a trusted third party such as a bank. There is no risk of repudiation or counterfeiting.

Learning about the bitcoin ledger was a eureka moment for me. I realized that bitcoin could enable permanent digital property rights on the internet. Even though I was convinced by the power and benefits of blockchain technology, I still did not yet fully comprehend how bitcoin could actually possess monetary value.

I needed to study the concept of monetary value.

Chapter 5: The Value and Function of Bitcoin

Value of Bitcoin

I understood and appreciated the capabilities and qualities of blockchain technology, which is what initially attracted me towards it, but I still could not bring myself to purchase any bitcoin because I was discouraged by the need to create a private cryptocurrency wallet to store bitcoin private keys. Holding your own private key is how owners of bitcoin can claim and spend their bitcoin on the blockchain.

The concept that monetary value could be stored within a digital token such as bitcoin on a cryptographically encrypted chain of blocks was still a challenging paradigm shift for me to make. I had cold feet, and I wasn't ready to make the commitment to jump on the bandwagon.

But much has improved since the fallout of QuadrigaCX (described earlier in Chapter 4). Cryptocurrency exchanges in Canada are now regulated, and the Ontario Securities Commission stated in their 2020 report that the failure of Quadriga was not indicative of the legitimacy of the cryptocurrency industry:

> *"Whether they were aware of it or not, Quadriga's clients were exposed to risks beyond fluctuations in crypto asset prices when they chose to trade on the Quadriga platform. Quadriga held and controlled their assets and misled them about the way those assets were being handled. Quadriga was not registered with any securities regulator. Cotten took advantage of this situation, treating his clients' assets as corporate or personal funds that he could spend, trade and*

use at will and ultimately depleting those assets to such an extent that he brought down the entire platform.

The misconduct we uncovered in relation to Quadriga is limited to Quadriga and should not be understood as applying to the crypto asset platform industry as a whole. Properly conducted, crypto asset trading is a legitimate and important component of our capital markets. We remain committed to working with this industry to foster innovation. Financial innovation has always been critical to the health of our economy and the competitiveness of our capital markets."[57]

Finally Convinced

In 2021, I was convinced that bitcoin was indeed money. I recognized that it could function as a store of value and a medium of exchange. I came to this conclusion while listening to the nine episodes of *The Saylor Series*[58] hosted by Robert Breedlove's, the *What is Money?* show. In these nine episodes, I learned many things about the history of money, gold, and bitcoin's thermodynamic properties.

According to the 1st law of thermodynamics, energy cannot be created or destroyed. Energy can only be transformed from one form to another. In this sense, when electrical energy is converted into computing power within a bitcoin-mining rig, the end result or output is the issuance of bitcoin within the distributed ledger.

Bitcoin is a revolutionary invention because bitcoin mining made it possible to capture electrical energy, work, and power in digital form. For the first time ever, energy, work, and power can be thought of as being embedded directly into a digital asset such as bitcoin, and it can be moved anywhere in the world over the internet in just a few minutes.

This excerpt taken from an article by Johannes Schweifer, explains why bitcoin possesses intrinsic value:

> *"It's funny, but true, to think that Bitcoin is also a store of the energy and resources that went into its creation, and that this fact contributes to its inherent, intrinsic value. It's a law of the universe that you can't just release that energy back into the air (or do something more 'meaningful' with it as some outspoken critics would say) in much the same way that you can't release all the energy embodied in gold by it's difficult production process. But still this value is there, because it saves you the same amount of time, energy, and resources needed today to mine it all over again yourself.*
>
> *This same fact goes for anything precious or valuable. The only important factor in the whole equation is how badly you need these precious things: Bitcoin, gold, platinum, etc. — it doesn't make a difference. Whether you need them for their properties as a currency, a medium of exchange, or for their inherent characteristics, is your own business. Most of the people who have no use for Bitcoin don't understand it, and the same can be said about gold. This makes gold and Bitcoin spiritual twins; one has been born into the physical world, the other into the digital."*[59]

This was my second eureka moment. I realized that for the first time, computer science and engineering intersected with money, finance, and economics. I was convinced that bitcoin possessed monetary value because it had captured energy in digital form, thereby enabling it to function as a medium of exchange and a store of value, just like gold. The only difference between bitcoin and gold is that the former has a digital nature and the latter has a physical one.

Money holds value if there is demand for it, which is largely determined by broad societal consensus. There is no reason why money has to exist solely in physical form. If software and algorithms can exist without physical form, and yet possess monetary value, then bitcoin's system of software, nodes, and a blockchain holding the distributed ledger of peer-to-peer transactions can also possess monetary value.

The internet has value because it can transport information across the globe in a matter of seconds. Bitcoin has value because it transports monetary value across the globe, on a cryptographically secured blockchain network, in a matter of minutes.

Once I arrived at the conclusion that bitcoin was truly money, I entered the proverbial *bitcoin rabbit hole*. While inside, I discovered what bitcoin truly was.

Bitcoin is a Protocol

In general terms, a protocol is a formal set of rules that governs the interaction between two parties. In the world of information technology and communication, a protocol is a standardized and defined set of formal rules describing how to transmit or exchange data across a network. For example, the internet protocol, TCP/IP,[60] enables the sending of packets of data across the internet, viewable using a web browser. Another example is the email protocol, SMTP,[61] which enables the sending and receiving of emails across the internet, viewable using an email client program, such as Gmail or Outlook.

Bitcoin is a protocol that enables direct peer-to-peer transactions between two parties without the need for a trusted 3rd party such as a bank. Spending bitcoin is similar to spending traditional currency and receiving change. The bitcoin protocol accomplishes this by executing the *unspent transaction output* (UTXO) protocol, which keeps track of how much bitcoin moves between the two parties involved in the transaction. The example below illustrates how UTXO works when Bob decides to send Alice 1 bitcoin (BTC):

> *"Let's say Bob has 1.2 BTC in his Bitcoin wallet. He*

wants to send 1 BTC to Alice. The network needs to recognize that Bob's wallet contains at least 1 BTC before the transaction can be processed. If Bob's wallet doesn't contain at least 1 BTC, then it should be impossible for him to send 1 BTC to Alice.

In the UTXO model, one or multiple unspent outputs may be added together to reflect the total amount of funds that belong to one user. In our example, Bob might have one UTXO worth 0.5 BTC and another worth 0.7 BTC, equaling to the total amount of funds in his Bitcoin wallet. When sending 1 BTC to Alice, Bob actually needs to send the entire amount of both UTXOs (1.2 BTC). Bob then receives one new UTXO containing 0.2 BTC. Meanwhile, Alice receives one new UTXO containing 1.0 BTC."[62]

Bitcoin is a Commodity

Like gold, bitcoin is a desirable and scarce commodity. In fact, many countries around the world already categorize bitcoin as a commodity for tax purposes. Bitcoin is already a legal commodity in the European Union, the US, Canada, Australia, Denmark, France, Germany, Iceland, Japan, Mexico, Spain, and the United Kingdom.

On September 7, 2021, El Salvador became the first country to make bitcoin legal tender. The Central African Republic soon followed in April 2022. Making bitcoin legal tender offers the hope of increasing the standard of living for the people in these countries.

Lugano, Switzerland also announced that bitcoin would become de facto legal tender, and on April 7th, 2022, the region of Honduras Prospera and Madeira in Portugal announced that they would adopt BTC as legal tender. In Argentina, citizens from the Mendoza Province can now pay government fees and taxes using cryptocurrencies[63].

Although bitcoin is often represented online as an orange-coloured or gold-coloured coin with the symbol, ₿, engraved on it, the actual digital reality of bitcoin is that it is not a coin or a discrete object which needs storage. Bitcoin is a monetary system operating by identical copies of the bitcoin core software on thousands of computer nodes in a network to secure a distributed ledger using blockchain technology. Bitcoin is simply a numerical value that gets issued by the software as a block reward to the successful bitcoin miner. The amount of bitcoin is recorded in the miner's account balance within the ledger.

Commodities are often considered to be scarce precious metals. Bitcoin is considered to be a digital commodity because it is scarce. The maximum number of bitcoins that will ever exist is 21 million. This hard cap will never be exceeded due to bitcoin's architecture, software, and incentive structure. If miners collectively try to increase the hard cap to more than 21 million bitcoins, then it would destroy the core investment proposition – its scarcity.

The bitcoin core software code is also very difficult to change because it would require the consensus of over half of the thousands of bitcoin nodes agreeing to a change, which is a highly improbable scenario. If there is any disagreement, it is possible for a new fork chain of bitcoin to be created, which could then compete with the original bitcoin blockchain.

This actually occurred in 2015 during the infamous block-size war.[64] There was a proposal to increase the block size to greater than 1 megabyte, but it was not supported by more than 50% of the bitcoin nodes. As a result, a new hard fork of bitcoin was created, which became known as Bitcoin Cash. It had a block-memory size of 8 megabytes. Bitcoin Cash was not fully adopted in the market, and so the original bitcoin blockchain continues to operate to this day with no change. This strength of the original bitcoin blockchain means that it is unlikely to have any competitors. This is another reason why bitcoin has been categorized as a commodity.

When all 21 million bitcoins have been mined in the year 2140, it will never be possible to mine any more. For this reason, bitcoin is even better than gold because it achieves absolute scarcity. Gold-mining production worldwide continues to increase as the demand for gold increases. No commodity exists today, other than bitcoin, with a fixed supply.

As the demand for bitcoin continues to get stronger over time as the available supply decreases, then this should cause the unit price of bitcoin to increase, meaning it will become more and more valuable over time.

Bitcoin is a Digital Asset

The genius of Satoshi Nakamoto's invention was that he created a decentralized and distributed database that uses the power of cryptography to securely store information in a way that permanently preserves the truth. The major achievement of this distributed database is that it prevents data from being modified or duplicated. It enables the permanent preservation of peer-to-peer transactions using bitcoin.

This is in stark contrast to the storage of information on centralized servers by companies such as Google and Amazon. When they store information, such as text, documents, audio, and video files, the data can be copied, saved, and altered by anyone. The centralized storage of information also increases the risk to the security and integrity of the information because it can more easily be targeted by hackers.

Decentralization is a much better strategy to protect and preserve the integrity of data. The reason why bitcoin works as a new monetary system is due to this invention of distributed ledger technology. The technology solved a well-known computer science problem in the field of distributed computing, known as the Byzantine Fault or the Byzantine Generals Problem[65].

This problem is typically described as being a game-theory problem faced by decentralized systems, which have no centralized command or master control. Imagine several generals surrounding the city of Byzantium, which they wish to attack and capture. The only way they can successfully besiege the city is to surround it and then attack it at the same time. If they attack at different times, they will fail.

The challenge is that the generals don't have any secure method of communicating with each other, and their messages can be intercepted by the Byzantium defenders. This means that the generals can never truly trust the authenticity of the messages that they receive. Since there is no option to centralize, the only way to solve this problem is to find a way to maintain a decentralized system, while coordinating the timing of the attack at the same time.

Bitcoin solved the problem by implementing a protocol that employs fault-tolerant mechanisms. This ensures that every general gets the same message without the need for a trusted third party, and without the generals needing to trust other generals. The network of generals are able to agree on the truth before it is recorded. If any general is unsure about the substance of the communication, the other generals can verify it using what they know to be true. It's a bit more complicated than this, but the bitcoin solution has been tried and tested in the computer science community, and it has never failed.

Solving the Byzantine Generals Problem is what enables the distributed ledger to permanently preserve the truth of bitcoin transactions with finality, and without the need for an intermediate third party. This is the technical reason why bitcoin exists, and why it has been so successful over the last 15 years.

About a year after the invention of bitcoin, the free market began to assign monetary value to bitcoin, and it became a digital asset. The very first bitcoin transaction occurred on May 22, 2010 when *"Laszlo Hanyecz paid Jeremy Sturdivant 10,000 bitcoins (BTC) for two Papa John's pizzas, which were delivered to Hanyecz's home."*[66] At that time, 10,000 bitcoins were worth about $40. Today, those 10,000 bitcoins would be worth about $400 million!

Non-fungible tokens (NFT) are a different kind of digital asset. They are being used to prove ownership of assets such as original pieces of digital art, music, and virtual plots of land. Technically, anything digital can be sold as an NFT.

The ownership of real world items, such as paintings and real estate are also being tokenized into NFTs. Even sub-cultures are becoming tokenized, for example, sports fans can purchase the crypto token, Chiliz, to gain voting rights on their favourite sports teams. Tokenization has become central to the future of the financial industry, and other cryptocurrencies such as ethereum will have a role to play with NFTs and smart contracts.

The internet has been a boon for internet companies and the economy in general over the past few decades. Blockchain technology is a natural next step in the evolution of the internet, and it has already sparked investment into new companies, new communities, new digital assets and new cryptocurrencies.

Some people believe that things will eventually evolve towards the creation of virtual cities and countries. Rather than thinking of a country or city requiring physical land, it is now possible to imagine a digital country or a digital city. This concept is also known as a network State, which has been well thought out and articulated by Balaji Srinivasan in his book, *The Network State: How to Start a New Country*[67], which is freely available online.

The author defines a network state as follows:

> *"A network state is a highly aligned online community*

with a capacity for collective action that crowdfunds territory around the world and eventually gains diplomatic recognition from pre-existing states." -- Balaji Srinivasan

Bitcoin is a Truth Machine

The bitcoin blockchain network is a truth machine[68]. Some consider it the *holy grail*[69] of individual sovereignty, eliminating the need for the traditional financial industry. It is an entirely new paradigm. The following list of quotes describes the significance of bitcoin:

- *"It's a truth machine. It's a way to eradicate all fraud or lying by human beings."* -- Dan Tapiero, Founder, CEO, CIO and Managing Partner of 10T Holdings
- *"Bitcoin is the most important invention in the history of the world since the Internet."* -- Roger Ver, bitcoin angel investor and evangelist
- *"Bitcoin is a remarkable cryptographic achievement, and the ability to create something that is not duplicable in the digital world has enormous value."* -- Eric Schmidt, CEO of Google
- *"Bitcoin will do to banks what email did to the postal industry."* -- Rick Falkvinge, Tech entrepreneur and founder of the Swedish Pirate Party
- *"Bitcoin may be the TCP/IP of money."* -- Paul Buchheit, creator of Gmail
- *"You can't stop things like Bitcoin. It will be everywhere and the world will have to readjust. World governments will have to readjust."* -- John McAfee, Founder of McAfee
- *"We have elected to put our money and faith in a mathematical framework that is free of politics and human error."* -- Tyler Winklevoss, Co-creator of Facebook

- *"Bitcoin is not unregulated. It is regulated by an algorithm instead of being regulated by government bureaucracies. Uncorrupted."* -- Andreas Antonopoulos, Blockchain expert
- *"Bitcoin will become the global asset settlement layer."* -- Mark Yusko, founder and chief investment officer of Morgan Creek Capital Management
- *"Bitcoin is a swarm of cyber hornets serving the goddess of wisdom, feeding on the fire of truth, exponentially growing ever smarter, faster, and stronger behind a wall of encrypted energy."* -- Michael Saylor, CEO of Micro Strategy
- *" Real estate cannot compete with bitcoin as a store of value. Bitcoin is rarer, more liquid, easier to move and harder to confiscate. It can be sent anywhere in the world at almost no cost at the speed of light. Real estate, on the other hand, is easy to confiscate and very difficult to liquidate in times of crisis. This was recently illustrated in Ukraine. After the Russian invasion on February 24, 2022, many Ukrainians turned to bitcoin to protect their wealth, bring their money with them, accept transfers and donations, and meet daily needs. Real estate, on the other hand, would have had to have been left behind."* -- Leon Wankum[70]

Many companies and large financial institutions, such as JP Morgan and Goldman Sachs, have already recognized that bitcoin is a new asset class, and they are already offering exposure to bitcoin and other digital assets to their clients.

In fact, within only one and a half decades, the digital assets industry has already amassed a market capitalization of approximately USD $2.15 trillion (as of April 3rd, 2022), which represents approximately 1/6th of the entire gold industry. Mr. Wonderful, Kevin O'Leary, said that the digital assets industry will one day become the 12th sector of the S&P 500 index[71].

Bitcoin could one day become a new world reserve asset or settlement layer, known as layer-1, on top of which other layer-2 cryptocurrencies could operate. If bitcoin becomes recognized as a new world reserve asset, then traditional currencies could eventually become a thing of the past. On December 26th, 2023, bitcoin was ranked #16 in the world's top currencies by market capitalization, and it was ranked #10 among the top assets in the world[72]. For this reason, bitcoin poses a threat to central and commercial banks.

Bitcoin is a monetary system for the people, and the impact of this is expected to be profound, especially in developing countries. A person only needs a cryptocurrency wallet installed on a cell phone or a computer connected to the internet in order to transact in bitcoin.

Bitcoin is for fairness, and it has the potential to enable self-sovereignty because bitcoin has no founder, no executive team, no marketing team, no paid development team, no ruling foundation, no insiders, no initial investors, no office, no website, and no human controlling it. Bitcoin is truly revolutionary as technology and money.

Chapter 6: Bitcoin is Unstoppable

The State Versus Bitcoin

Bitcoin first appeared on the internet on January 3, 2009, and since then it has never been hacked or compromised in any way. It is censorship resistant, meaning that third parties cannot prevent transactions from occurring, and they can't confiscate or modify bitcoin in any way. The bitcoin ledger holds the truth of every transaction ever made, and it is openly available for viewing on the internet.[73]

Because of these features and the continued success of bitcoin, governments are worried that people will prefer bitcoin over government-issued local currencies. If this happens, then the central banking system and its network of commercial banks will become less relevant. A battle between government-issued currencies and bitcoin has already begun.

Someone once said, "First they ignore you, then they laugh at you, then they fight you, then you win." This statement applies to technologies such as bitcoin, a potential disruptor of the existing State-controlled system.

At first, the State completely ignored cryptocurrency in the early years of bitcoin. It was dismissed as a fringe digital phenomenon or a passing fad. A few years later, when the State started to learn more about bitcoin, they laughed at it, and called it a scam. By 2020, after the State discovered that bitcoin could function as real money, politicians and regulators began to fight it through regulation and legal court battles.

Propaganda campaigns were soon launched by governments to discourage the public from investing in cryptocurrency, and these campaigns continue in full force[74]. The European Central Bank published an article[75] and a blog[76] about the failed promises of bitcoin in an attempt to discredit the entire cryptocurrency industry. Most recently, in the US, Jamie Dimon, CEO of JPMorgan, stated at a Senate Committee on Banking that: *"The only true use case for it is criminals, drug traffickers, money laundering, tax avoidance, ... if I were the government, I'd close it down."*[77]

This statement by Jamie Dimon was untruthful. To the surprise of many, shortly after his statement at the Senate Committee hearing, his company was named as an authorized participant for several proposed spot bitcoin exchange traded funds (ETF).[78] Why would JPMorgan knowingly participate in something he believed to be used for criminal activity?

The existence of this kind of propaganda against cryptocurrency is a sign of a new paradigm shift on the horizon.

In fact, more financial crimes are committed with traditional currencies rather than with bitcoin. Traditional currencies are much easier to conceal by criminals. The use of bitcoin can't be concealed because law enforcement can easily trace bitcoin transactions on the open blockchain (discussed later in more detail in Chapter 7).

The government of China attempted to ban bitcoin on multiple occasions in recent years without any success.[79] In 2021, China banned bitcoin mining operations throughout the country, but the miners just packed up their mining rigs and left to operate and thrive in other countries, such as the US and Canada. Time and time again, bitcoin has proven itself to be anti-fragile, and the State hasn't been able to destroy it. There is literally no off switch.

When El Salvador declared bitcoin as legal tender in 2021, the International Monetary Fund (IMF) warned and urged president Nayib Bukele to reverse course. The IMF even threatened El Salvador by stating it would be difficult for El Salvador to get a future loan from the IMF[80]. Fortunately, Bukele was not deterred, and he dismissed the IMF's threats[81]. President Bukele was ahead of his time.

We are now in the last stages of the battle against bitcoin and cryptocurrency in general. I believe that bitcoin will prevail. Bitcoin is the first decentralized digital asset to be free from State coercion or manipulation because there is no central authority that can be attacked.

These examples of opposition to bitcoin are signs that the traditional financial industry is worried. If bitcoin becomes a new world reserve asset, then many pundits believe that barrels of oil could one day be priced in bitcoin rather than in US dollars.

Moving to a new bitcoin standard would put an end to government manipulation of currencies. Imagine a world without monetary inflation and debasement of currency! The politically neutral nature of bitcoin will make international trade more fair. No country left behind!

Bitcoin's Competition

Gold has been a store of value for thousands of years. It is considered valuable for reasons such as jewelry making, electrical components, and dental work. Gold is valuable because it is scarce and hard to find. It takes a considerable amount of time and energy to mine it out of the ground.

This combination of high demand and scarcity, along with the high amounts of energy needed to mine gold out of the ground, has given rise to gold's status as a universal store of value. Gold coins were first used as a medium of exchange over 2000 years ago during the 6th Century BC in Lydia, now a part of Western Turkey. Gold coins were also used in China, dating back to 700 BC[82].

To evaluate how good money can be, it should have some basic properties. It should be durable so that it can last a long time, divisible so that it can be used to make payments accurately, recognizable so that people are willing to accept it, portable so that it can easily be carried or moved from one place to another across space and time, and scarce so that it maintains its monetary value over time. If all of these properties and more are strong, then the money will be considered to be good or *hard*. But if one or more of these properties are weak, then the money wouldn't be that useful, and it would be considered to be bad or *soft*.

But how does bitcoin compare to other forms of money? It is possible to evaluate bitcoin by comparing it to the properties of money just described. Figure 4 compares bitcoin to gold and the US dollar. Bitcoin wins on every property. Michael Saylor and Robert Breedlove make a very convincing case that all of the properties of money have been perfected by bitcoin, and they have referred to it as digital gold[83]. I think they are right.

Properties of Money	Precious Metal e.g. gold	Traditional Currency e.g. US dollar	Bitcoin
Fungible (interchangeable)	high	high	high
Portable	moderate	high	high
Durable	high	moderate	high
Highly Divisible	moderate	moderate	high
Counterfeit Resistant	moderate	moderate	high
Easily Transactable	low	high	high
Scarce (predictable supply)	moderate	low	high
Inflation Resistant	high	low	high
Decentralized	low	low	high
Smart (programmable)	low	low	high
Open Source	low	low	high
Irreversible Payments	low	low	high

Figure 4 – A comparison of the properties of gold, the US dollar, and bitcoin

According to Figure 4, bitcoin scores highest on every property. It is no wonder why it is being recognized as digital gold. This is the likely reason why some governments already consider bitcoin to be a commodity.

Although security is not one of the properties mentioned in Figure 4, it is very important to consider. America's gold reserves are safely stored and secured at Fort Knox in the state of Kentucky and within bank vaults around the world. Currencies are also securely stored in bank vaults around the world.

Bitcoin, however, has no need for a vault or a specialized building such as Fort Knox. Bitcoin is inherently secured on a blockchain, and thousands of identical copies of the bitcoin ledger are stored on a decentralized network of computers all around the world . Having multiple copies ensures its integrity and resistance to tampering. In fact, bitcoin never actually leaves the blockchain, and so it can't be confiscated.

Unlike gold and currency, bitcoin's ownership is controlled by cryptographic private keys. Imagine if every holding of a gold coin or US dollar had a key belonging to the owner! With bitcoin, only the owner of the private key is capable of claiming it and sending it as payment to others. The movement of bitcoin occurs within the bitcoin ledger itself.

Anyone with a public bitcoin address can receive bitcoin. Think of a bitcoin public address as your own personal mailbox, with the condition that anyone can see the mailbox address, but they can't look inside to determine what's in it. The only way to send bitcoin is for the owner to use their private key to open the mailbox and send some bitcoin to someone else.

Over 100 governments around the world are attempting to compete with bitcoin by considering the creation of central bank digital currencies (CBDC). For example, China was the first to launch its own CBDC, which is not surprising given the Chinese government's surveillance mentality and privacy violations of its own citizens[84]. This aligns with China's social credit system because it enables the government to know exactly what was sold and purchased, and the parties involved in every transaction.

Fortunately, the US does not have a CBDC as it would need Congressional approval to do so.[85] However, the US Federal Reserve has been working on a project called, FedNow, in an attempt to compete with bitcoin. Similar but now quite a CBDC, FedNow claims to offer a new payment infrastructure that will allow financial institutions across America to provide instant financial settlement. The Fed claims that the FedNow system will not give them the power to monitor, freeze, or seize private bank accounts based on a person's behaviour or political beliefs. However, this is a matter of trust, and as long as trust is needed within the traditional financial system, it will continue to perpetuate corruption.

Only a trustless and codified decentralized monetary system such as bitcoin, can provide a trustworthy monetary system. Fortunately, American politicians such as, Ron DeSantis (Republican) and Robert F. Kennedy Jr. (Democrat), have both opposed the FedNow program, sounding the alarm bells about the threat of "ultimate mechanisms for social surveillance and control".[86]

Transition to Bitcoin Begins

As long as energy is available to create electricity, and as long as the internet continues to operate on personal devices, such as a computer or cell phone, then bitcoin has the potential to become a major world reserve asset.

Some people believe that barrels of oil could one day be denominated in bitcoin[87]. If bitcoin becomes a significant world reserve asset, then it will be accessible to over a billion people in the world who currently don't have access to financial services.

It is quite probable that within a few short years, most governments around the world will embrace bitcoin as an important technology, ushering in a new era of decentralized finance. The benefit of using bitcoin is that it will direct more wealth and purchasing power back into the hands of the working class.

The Security Exchange Commission (SEC), under the leadership of Gary Gensler, was very slow to approve a spot bitcoin ETF in the US, but it finally approved several of them on January 10, 2024.

During 2022 and 2023, some fraudulent actors in the cryptocurrency exchange and cryptocurrency lending platform spaces were apprehended and prosecuted. As a result, bitcoin's unique position as the dominant digital asset relative to all other cryptocurrencies continues to rise. In 2023, bitcoin dominated as the best-performing asset. It surged over 150% within that one year. This sparked considerable interest among the world's largest investment firms, such as BlackRock, which controls approximately $10 trillion of assets under management.

Larry Fink, the Chief Executive Officer of BlackRock, believes that crypto is a *"flight to quality"*. He also said: *"Crypto is digitizing gold in many ways"* and *"Bitcoin is an international asset."*[88] After recent SEC approval of spot bitcoin ETFs, Larry Fink then went on to say: "We believe this is just the beginning. ETFs are step one in the technological revolution in the financial markets. Step two is going to be the tokenization of every financial asset."[89]

Jurrien Timmer, the head of macro at Fidelity Investments, recently claimed that: *"...bitcoin is a commodity currency that aspires to be a store of value and a hedge against monetary debasement. I think of it as exponential gold."*[90]

Tim Draper, venture capitalist and founder of Draper Associates, recently claimed that: *"Bitcoin solves inflation permanently."*[91]

In 2023, Gary Gensler and the SEC lost their case against Ripple Labs, Inc., accusing it of conducting a USD $1.3 billion offering of unregistered securities using the digital asset, XRP. The judge ruled in favor of XRP, and deemed it to have the status of a commodity rather than a security in certain cases. This was a huge land-mark win for the entire cryptocurrency industry at large, and so the path to cryptocurrency adoption continues to magnify despite opposition by the State.

Failure of Keynesian Economics

I was surprised to learn that in 1971, the United States of America made the decision to break away from the gold standard, and at the same time it decided to adopt the principles of Keynesian economics rather than Austrian economics. This travesty is well explained by Saifedean Ammous in his famous 2018 book, *The Bitcoin Standard*.

By breaking the relationship between the US dollar and gold, there would no longer be a limit as to how many US dollars could be printed by the US government. It could simply print and issue as many new dollars as it wanted, by fiat, a Latin word meaning *it shall be*.

Since then, we now call the US dollar and all other government-issued currencies in the world, fiat currency, because they have come into existence by decree, without any proof-of-work system, i.e., no energy was spent to do the hard work of mining for precious metals such as gold to back the dollar. The only reason why fiat currencies today have any value at all is due to the government saying that it does.

Governments and their central banks have full control over the money supply and interest rates in their respective countries, and this has caused the problem of inflation. In some countries, inflation has reached a point where the fiat currency has become worthless, thus inflicting poverty on its citizens.

Unfortunately, Keynesian economic theory has influenced most developed countries around the world. The governments in these countries have full control of the economy through active management and regulation of an intentional elastic money supply and modifiable interest rates. These governments believe that their intervention is necessary in order to stabilize the economy. They use Keynesian economics to justify their actions.

Stabilization of economies has clearly not been achieved in any country. Stock markets continue to undergo boom and bust cycles. When the government interferes with the economy it distorts the prices of goods and services to such a degree that it makes it difficult for individuals and businesses to plan for their future.

The Keynesian experiment has been a failure in my view, and the proof of that is in the observed debasement of currencies caused by an increase in the money supply. This results in a loss of purchasing power, i.e., inflation and hyperinflation.

When a currency's purchasing power continues to decrease, it becomes more difficult for people to afford goods and services. For example, today it is next to impossible for the Millennial generation to purchase a house to live in without taking on a lot of debt. In fact, America is currently in a consumer debt crisis, whether it be debt taken on for a home, automobile, student loan, or credit card[92].

The opposite of Keynesian economics is Austrian economics, which favours limited to no government intervention in the economy. It views money as inelastic, such that the money supply and interest rates are not manipulated by a central bank or government, and are rather left up to the free market to determine.

Austrian economists believe that the free market is better at adapting and responding to economic conditions, and that businesses should be allowed to fail as a necessary feature of the system. In such an economy, the money would be stable and sound, as it used to be when the US dollar was backed by gold.

The Austrian economist, Friedrich Hayek, described in his

seminal paper, *The Use of Knowledge in Society*[93], that prices operating in a free market economy actually function in a way to transmit the maximal amount of information in just a few digits. Prices convey enough information to people, allowing them to make informed decisions. The more closely prices match the actual costs, the better decisions people are able to make.

For example, if the price of some good or service goes up, this would be sufficient information for the consumer to make a decision. There could be thousands of reasons to cause prices to increase, but a buyer only needs to know whether it is worth it to them to purchase the good or service at the given price or not. In this way, prices are free to adjust according to the forces of supply and demand such that producers will be able to figure out whether they need to produce more or less of something, while adjusting their prices to maximize their profits and reduce their losses.

The entire system is decentralized and works optimally without any central planning. In this way, the coordination of resource allocation, production, price signals, and the forces of supply and demand all function optimally, analogous to the way starlings flock together in murmurations.[94] If you haven't yet observed a murmuration, I highly recommend it. Despite the close proximity of the birds in flight, they never crash into each other, and yet beautiful and harmonious patterns emerge.

Rather than having the US dollar return to the gold standard, bitcoin is a better solution overall because of its better properties, as previously shown in Figure 4. Also, bitcoin has a fixed supply of 21 million, which can never be manipulated by any individual or government.

Given the current problem of inflation around the world, digital assets such as bitcoin have the potential to offer billions of people, who are either bankless or underbanked, a secure and reliable way of participating in the economy. This is especially true for citizens in developing countries or in war-torn countries and dictatorships.

Bitcoin can help these individuals to protect their wealth against government oppression or hyperinflation. In Turkey for example, 50% of its citizens have turned to bitcoin and other cryptocurrencies as a safe haven[95]. This is a prime example where adoption of hard money, such as bitcoin, has the potential to fix the problem.

"Fix the money, fix the world."[96] -- G. Edward Griffin

"Bitcoin fixes the government monopoly of money and currency debasement."[97] -- Dylan LeClair

"Crypto will transcend any one currency."[98] -- Larry Fink, CEO of BlackRock, the world's largest asset manager

Chapter 7: Morality of Money

Is Money the Root of All Evil?

Money is just a tool or technology, but it clearly comes with moral and ethical implications. We have all heard the old cliché that money is the root of all evil, but is this really true? I think the better and more accurate understanding about the morality of money was written by St. Paul in his first letter to Timothy from the New Testament of the Bible, in which he said: *"For the **love** of money is the root of all evils; it is through this craving that some have wandered away from the faith and pierced their hearts with many pangs."*[99]

The Catholic Church teaches that greed is one of the seven deadly sins. In the context of money (within a healthy monetary system), greed is a disordered love of riches, such that the love of money becomes elevated above the love of God or neighbour. In other words, greed becomes a deadly sin when money becomes idolized, thus breaking the first commandment, which states: *"You shall have no other gods before me."*[100]

Jesus reinforced this point when he said:

> *"Truly, I say to you, it will be hard for a rich man to enter the kingdom of heaven. Again I tell you, it is easier for a camel to go through the eye of a needle than for a rich man to enter the kingdom of God."*[101]

Jesus asked the rich man to sell his possessions and give them to the poor before following him. The rich man couldn't do it, and he *"went away sorrowful."*[102] Christians understand this teaching to mean that amassing great wealth and riches is not a sin in itself, as long as the rich person does not become a slave to money and can part with it. A great example of this is in the parable of the

Widow's Offering when Jesus makes the point about the poor woman giving more than the rich man:

> *And he sat down opposite the treasury, and watched the multitude putting money into the treasury. Many rich people put in large sums. And a poor widow came, and put in two copper coins, which make a penny. And he called his disciples to him, and said to them, "Truly, I say to you, this poor widow has put in more than all those who are contributing to the treasury. For they all contributed out of their abundance; but she out of her poverty has put in everything she had, her whole living."*[103]

Another commandment that most people are aware of is: *"You shall not steal."*[104] As long as money has existed, there have been those who are tempted to steal.

Traditional government-issued currencies account for the great majority of crimes. For example, India suffered its greatest banking heist in 2018 when the Punjab National Bank was defrauded USD $1.8 billion by the companies operated by diamond tycoon, Nirav Modi[105].

In the last 15 years, criminals have attempted to exploit digital assets such as bitcoin to commit crimes, but they are getting caught. They are getting caught because of the open and transparent nature of blockchain ledgers. These ledgers record all transactions made using digital assets or cryptocurrencies, and this has allowed law enforcement officials to use sophisticated chain analysis tools to apprehend thieves.

By using on-chain analytics, investigators are able to track the movement of digital assets from one public address to another, which eventually leads them to the criminal[106]. Apprehending criminals is possible because of the transparency of the blockchain, which allows for easier traceability.

With bitcoin it is impossible to counterfeit money unlike government-issued paper notes and coin denominations. For this reason, I believe that the use of digital assets and cryptocurrencies will have a net positive impact on society by reducing financial crimes.

It may be more accurate to say that today's traditional monetary system, with its government-issued currencies, is the root of all evil. In our current financial system, the rules of the game are often manipulated by central banks and governments, thus making it difficult for the common person to maintain and grow wealth.

An analogy that may help to understand why the rules of a game need to be consistent and predictable is to consider the sport of soccer (football for most of the world). It has well-defined rules, and all players understand them. Football fans can enjoy the game precisely because they know that the game is always played according to its fixed set of rules and without any outside interference. There is a reliable sense of impartiality, fairness and justice, win or lose.

But imagine if during the course of the game, the rules suddenly changed on a whim, or if the referee decided to favour one team and penalize the other for no logical reason. Suddenly the game would become unfair and chaotic. This kind of game would be considered evil because the outcome of the game would be determined by the referees rather than being based on the merit and performance of the players themselves.

In today's traditional financial system, the government is like an unfair referee, modifying the rules of the game on a whim. This causes immense suffering to businesses, investors and consumers. For example, there are times when government officials or central banks suddenly decide to print more money, raise or lower taxes, or raise or lower interest rates. They have also bailed out banks and businesses that they favour during economic crises, to the point where these institutions can never fail, regardless of their performance.

It is this kind of sick financial system that gave rise to the 2008 financial crisis. During the crisis, the US government spent USD $700 billion to bail out 991 institutions, such as AIG Insurance, General Motors, Citigroup, Bank of America, JPMorgan Chase, Wells Fargo, Chrysler, Morgan Stanley, Goldman Sachs, just to name a few. When governments do this, it destroys the game, making it an unfair and uneven playing field.

When governments provide these kinds of bailouts, it also results in the devaluation or debasement of the currency, effectively punishing the poor and rewarding the wealthy. For this reason, I believe that the existing financial system is corrupt. It is the natural outcome of Keynesian economics.

When the government favours some businesses over others it results in the old adage, *the rich get richer, and the poor get poorer*. Imagine having to play football while the size of the field increased without any warning during the game, making it harder and harder to score. On top of that, imagine if the referee favoured one team over the other, and changed the rules to help their own favoured team to win. This is exactly what happens when governments have control over the fiat currency rule book.

There are many examples of failed traditional financial systems. Consider a country such as Venezuela, which has the largest oil reserves in the world, slightly more than Saudi Arabia[107]. Venezuela used to be one of the wealthiest nations in the world in the 1960s, not so far behind the United States, but today it is one of the poorest. From 2013 to 2018, inflation in Venezuela rose from 41% to 65,000% primarily due to the manipulation of monetary policy by Hugo Chávez. In 2017, the government increased the money supply by 14%, and unemployment rose to over 20%, similar to the Great Depression in the US. Another cause of inflation was the Chávez government's regulation of price controls for food and medicine. His mandated prices were so low that companies went out of business. This caused higher unemployment, and in response, the government had to pay more to import goods, and when the money ran out, the government started printing more money. This vicious cycle led to an annual inflation rate of 2,300% in early 2020, and the economy completely collapsed[108].

Venezuela is a classic example where central planning and manipulation of monetary policy resulted in the destruction of its fiat currency, the bolivar. Wheelbarrows of bolivars in large sacks of cash were needed just to purchase a loaf of bread[109].

Whenever hyperinflation occurs, currencies lose their value over time, and since wages don't typically keep up with inflation, it translates to getting a pay cut every time the government decides to print more money. Since 2008, Venezuela's central bank actually had to slash 14 zeroes off its currency to simplify transactions for the most basic goods and services. A 2019 article in *Business Insider* magazine stated that the country was considered to be in a state of economic crisis due to corruption and failed government policies. This left millions of Venezuelans in poverty[110].

Because fiat currencies are prone to inflation, it is a terrible method of storing monetary value. I would go so far as to say that the entire financial system, which is based on fiat currency, is broken because it is manipulated by governments. For this reason I think fiat currencies are the root of all evil.

Fortunately, we now have bitcoin, which is the complete opposite of fiat currency. I would say that the answer to the question, *Is money the root of all evil?*, is *no*; but it depends on the context as per the following statements:

1. Bitcoin <u>is not</u> the root of all evil. It is a rules-based and unchangeable monetary system that always remains fair and just.

2. Fiat currency <u>is</u> the root of all evil because it can be manipulated by the State.

3. The <u>love</u> of fiat currency <u>is</u> the root of all evil when it becomes idolized.

4. The <u>love</u> of bitcoin <u>is</u> the root of all evil when it becomes

idolized.

5. The desire for wealth and obtaining it is not evil when your wealth is used to serve your fellow man, and when it is used to promote goodness, beauty, and truth in the world.

If our financial system operated under the Austrian school of economics, then there would be no government bailouts, and the rules of the game would remain fixed and fair, based on the rule of law. When the rules of the game are fixed and reliable, as is the case with bitcoin, then the individual has the responsibility to make decisions on how best to spend or save their bitcoin.

Bitcoin can't eliminate wickedness and sin from people, but it has already proven that it is a better technology than government-issued currency. Bitcoin offers the hope of reducing financial crimes, making it more reliable and trustworthy. This would bring hope to the individual, and the cumulative effect could be to improve living standards and the quality of life within entire nations.

Bitcoin is for Fairness

Order emerges from fixed and unchangeable systems, not from central planning by committees[111]. This is why bitcoin offers so much hope. It was programmed to be a perfectly decentralized and permissionless monetary system without the possibility of any central body changing the rules. It operates on a fixed set of programmatic rules to allow the game to be played fairly by anyone and everyone. The bitcoin software that runs the system is not subject to any central authority because no such authority exists.

Bitcoin can be used as a store of value and a medium of exchange while its blockchain keeps track of all transactions on an immutable and decentralized ledger. It is the perfect peer-to-peer electronic payment system on the internet without the need for a trusted intermediary.

Because no government can influence or control the total supply of bitcoin, it can never be inflated, thus retaining its value over time. Only the dynamics of supply and demand will determine its price on the market.

Using bitcoin also prevents any central body from freezing the asset because bitcoin always resides on the blockchain, which has never been hacked since bitcoin's inception. As long as the owners of bitcoin hold their private keys in a personal cryptocurrency wallet, their bitcoin is safely secured on the blockchain.

In the current fiat system, the government can extend its powers to order banks or centralized cryptocurrency exchanges to freeze the flow of money to and from an individual's bank account for any reason. This happened in Canada when the Freedom Convoy[112] exercised its democratic right to freely assemble and demonstrate against COVID-19 vaccine mandates[113].

It was impossible for the government to shut down or freeze the bitcoin network due to its decentralized nature, but the government was able to go after the centralized cryptocurrency exchanges. Because of the centralized nature of these exchanges, the government was able to force the exchanges to freeze the assets of certain individuals, who left their private keys on the exchange.

Had the private keys been taken off of the centralized cryptocurrency exchanges the government would not have been able to freeze the assets. This could have easily been done by storing an individual's private keys in a private cryptocurrency wallet.

If nations adopt and use bitcoin as the primary digital asset to be used as a medium of exchange and store of value, then it will likely help poor and developing countries with hyperinflation or high inflation to get back on track. The citizens of these countries will then have the hope of saving their wealth in a perfect, non-inflationary monetary environment, free from government manipulation.

Anyone who decides to transact using bitcoin can now become their own bank. The impact of this is significant. It means that the world's bankless or underbanked population of 1.6 billion people[114] can have access to money and financial products as long as they have a cell phone or a computer connected to the internet. This makes for a more a fair and just financial system for everyone.

Be Your Own Bank – Creative Disruption

To be your own bank is a fascinating concept, which is now possible with cryptocurrency. Managing your own money without a commercial bank will require your own private non-custodial cryptocurrency wallet. This kind of wallet is freely available in various forms depending on your needs, and they are often categorized as being either *hot* or *cold* wallets. A hot wallet can be downloaded as software onto your cell phone or computer, while it always remains connected to the internet, and a cold wallet is a hardware device, similar to a USB key, that is specialized in storing your private keys offline, even if the device is connected to the internet.

A hot wallet should be used when storing small amounts of bitcoin, such as a couple of hundreds of dollars worth, and a cold wallet should be used when storing larger amounts that you don't plan on using for several months or years. The private keys stored on a hardware wallet never leave the device, so that you are always in control.

Using a cryptocurrency wallet effectively frees a person from relying on a bank, and it promotes individual sovereignty. Many consider this to be a huge improvement over the traditional banking system because it enables people to send and receive any amount of money across the world, almost instantly, without the need for the services of a commercial bank. Payment systems such as Interac, PayPal or Venmo are no longer needed.

Owning a cryptocurrency wallet would enable approximately 1.6 billion people around the world, who are either underbanked or bankless, to be included in the financial system. Such individuals could begin saving their wealth in bitcoin, which would offer them hope for a better future.

This concept of being your own bank has become very relevant, even in America. Recently in April 2023, two traditional banks collapsed entirely: Silicon Valley Bank and Signature Bank, the third-largest bank failure in US history. After their collapse, record levels of deposit poured into Bank of America, JPMorgan Chase, and Citibank.[115]

Republican Senator for North Carolina, Ted Budd, introduced a new bill called the *Keep Your Coins Act*, which would protect an individual's right to conduct transactions with digital assets without the need for an intermediate third party. He stated:

> *"As consumers face new challenges and risks associated with the use of digital currencies, we should be empowering individuals to maintain control over their own digital assets. This approach will foster financial freedom and a more decentralized cryptocurrency ecosystem."*[116]

As more people adopt digital assets to store monetary value and to transact with digital assets as a medium of exchange, then traditional financial institutions such as commercial banks, and credit-card companies are at risk of losing customers. The disruptive nature of digital assets is forcing these institutions to either adapt by offering similar services to their customers, or face the risk of losing their customers altogether.

Anyone can now use bitcoin's system of public addresses to complete transactions in a peer-to-peer manner. The only time a bitcoin public address is associated to a person's name and their personally identifiable information is on a cryptocurrency exchange.

In Canada, for example, many cryptocurrency exchanges are approved and regulated for use, but they require the collection of *know your customer* information. In order to make a digital asset purchase using fiat currency, you'll need to provide your true identity when setting up an account with the exchange.

Today, cryptocurrency exchanges are still centralized, and they are legally required to acquire and store your identification and home-address information before allowing you to purchase and trade cryptocurrencies. So even though the bitcoin network is fully decentralized and bitcoin public addresses are anonymous, the government could compel a cryptocurrency exchange to reveal the identity of a person's bitcoin public address.

New decentralized cryptocurrency exchanges (DEX) are being tested, and they will operate in a way to enable the purchase of digital assets without having to collect and store personally identifiable information.

When a person uses a centralized cryptocurrency exchange to purchase bitcoin with fiat currency, the exchange will store the bitcoin private key within the exchange's custodial wallet to prove the ownership of a unique bitcoin public address. While the private key is stored inside the exchange's custodial wallet associated to an individual's account, there is always an option to withdraw the private keys to a private non-custodial cryptocurrency wallet. This action will allow a person to fully control their own private keys, and thus the bitcoin, effectively becoming their own bank!

Many people prefer this option rather than trusting the exchange to store their private keys; however, some people may decide to trust the exchange's custodial wallet services if they are worried about losing their own private keys themselves. Depending on your situation, this may be desirable.

Many exchanges today are insured and use strongly secured multi-signature custodial wallets to keep private keys safe[117].

However, as mentioned earlier, the government will always be able to compel a centralized exchange to freeze assets as long as the exchange continues to hold the private keys. For this reason it is always recommended to remove your private keys off of a centralized exchange, and store them in your own private cryptocurrency wallet.

Bitcoin Mining is Green

Environmentalists argue that the energy consumption needed to secure the bitcoin network is so high that it is similar to the energy consumption of some countries. For this reason, they believe that it is irresponsible to use so much energy to mine bitcoin. I believe that this kind of sentiment is misinformed. In actual fact, bitcoin is a very important technology that can help to stabilize power grids, and its use of renewable energy is higher than what most people think.

Comparing the energy usage of bitcoin to the energy consumption of a country is not really a fair comparison because it is not comparing apples to apples. It would be more accurate and fair to compare the energy consumption of bitcoin to the amount of energy used to mine gold or to run the existing banking industry.

Estimating the energy consumption of these industries was calculated in a report by Galaxy Digital[118] in May 2021. In their report, the total electricity consumption of the bitcoin network was estimated in terra watt (TW) hours per year to be less than half of the electricity consumption of the gold mining industry and the banking industry:

- 263.72 TWh/year to operate bank data centres, branches, ATMs, and card network data centres

- 240.61 TWh/year to run gold mining, milling, smelting, and refining operations, not including oil used to produce rubber tires, e.g., Barrick Gold consumed 25,000 tons of rubber tires in 2013

- 113.89 TWh/year to operate bitcoin mining rigs, mining pools, and the tens of thousands of nodes making up the blockchain network

Based on these results, it is clear that gold mining and the banking industry expend far more energy than bitcoin mining per year. It would be better for environmentalists to lobby against the energy consumption of the gold industry or the banking industry, and acknowledge that bitcoin is a greener alternative.

Bitcoin has also proven itself to be a green technology because it is remarkable at transitioning from the use of fossil fuels to using renewable energy sources such as hydro, wind, solar, and geothermal energy from volcanoes. A May 2023 report in Forbes magazine reported bitcoin's global energy consumption from renewable sources to be well over 50%:

> *"In Q4 2022, the global consortium Bitcoin Mining Council indicated that 58.9% of the global energy consumption associated with bitcoin mining comes from renewables."*[119]

El Salvador, for example, uses power harnessed from green geothermal energy sources emitted from the Santa Ana volcano to mine bitcoin blocks and earn bitcoin rewards. The government has also recently announce that it will invest USD $1 billion to build one of the world's largest mining farms powered by a 241 MW power generation park using solar and wind energy in the northwestern municipality of Metapan.[120]

In the United States of America some bitcoin miners are capturing and reusing flared gas emitted from waste methane at oil wells. By locating mining rigs close to oil wells, bitcoin miners have been able to pipe the wasted flared gas to generators in order to produce the electricity needed to power bitcoin mining rigs. This means that bitcoin mining can actually help to reduce pollution!

Power utilities have realized that when partnered with bitcoin mining farms, they have been able to achieve better grid stability. Because bitcoin miners have no customers, and no function other than executing the SHA-256 hash function to successfully mine and validate bitcoin blocks on the blockchain, they are capable of shutting down for extended periods of time whenever the power grid is on the verge of being destabilized. By using sophisticated software to control the mining rigs during peak demand periods, the power grid can be stabilized.

Most other businesses and customers of power utilities are not able to do this because they have very stringent down-time requirements in order to serve their customers. Power hungry companies such as Google and Facebook always have to be operational 24 hours per day, 7 days per week.

Bitcoin mining farms on the other hand do not have this requirement, and they are the perfect customer for power utilities. When partnered together: *"Bitcoin enables mining utilities to engage in agreements that are mutually beneficial to miners and the electricity grid."*[121]

When bitcoin miners are successful at validating blocks on the bitcoin blockchain, the bitcoin core software issues new bitcoin into the system as a reward to the miners. The agreements between bitcoin miners and power utilities are mutually beneficial because they help miners to obtain electricity at an agreed cost, and they help power utilities to stabilize the power grid for its customers.

The benefit of using energy to mine bitcoin is that it results in an unbreakable and tamper-proof decentralized ledger that holds the truth of every peer-to-peer transaction. Achieving the final truth on a network is the real reason why bitcoin has achieved the status of a digital asset possessing monetary value.

Without the use of energy, it would not have been possible to create such a trustworthy monetary network worth almost a trillion dollars. As of December 26, 2023, the bitcoin monetary network was worth USD $822 billion. The use of energy to create a trillion dollar cryptocurrency industry (bitcoin plus all other alt-coins) created all of this tremendous value [19.58 million bitcoins X USD $42,000 per bitcoin = USD $822 billion].

Burning Fossil Fuels is a Moral Imperative

I agree with Alex Epstein[122] who believes that humanity should accelerate its harnessing of energy from fossil fuels, such as oil, natural gas, and coal while improving technologies to help reduce environmental pollution.

The earth has an abundance of energy sources to help improve our quality of life and human flourishing. The energy from fossil fuels is greatly needed in poor nations that don't have the luxury of clean running water and the infrastructure required to provide human dignity and the opportunities that we take for granted in the West.

If you are reading this book, you most likely live in a fully developed country with all of the infrastructure already built, e.g., homes, schools, hospitals, factories, airports, railways, trains, planes, automobiles, etc., and with all of the necessary medicines to promote healthy and long productive lives.

The fact is, the only way to alleviate poverty and to improve the life expectancy of billions of people in poor nations around the world is to continue using more fossil fuels, the cheapest and most abundantly available energy source that the earth provides. According to Alex Epstein: *"3 billion people… still use less electricity than a typical American refrigerator…to allow them to have a modern life, that's going to depend on fossil fuels."*

Over the last few decades, China and India have been able to lift millions of people out of poverty precisely because they have been able to use energy from fossil fuels to increase productivity.

This increase in productivity has provided more goods and services to support the masses. I believe it is a moral imperative to continue extracting energy from fossil fuels to help improve the lives and living conditions for everyone.

The Catholic Church, in its wisdom, also supports this view of using the earth's resources to provide for the needs of man. This was best explained in *Rerum Novarum*, the 1891 Encyclical by Pope Leo XIII on Capital and Labor[123]. In this encyclical, the Catholic Church expressed its opposition to socialism, and instead favoured the notion that the individual, not the State, should possess the fruits of the earth.

Pope Leo XIII strongly denounced the socialist agenda for striving to do away with private property, and he was against the idea that individual possessions should become the common property of all and administered by the State. He referred to such policies as unjust:

> *"... emphatically unjust, for they would rob the lawful possessor, distort the functions of the State, and create utter confusion in the community... Socialists, therefore, by endeavoring to transfer the possessions of individuals to the community at large, strike at the interests of every wage-earner, since they would deprive him of the liberty of disposing of his wages, and thereby of all hope and possibility of increasing his resources and of bettering his condition in life. Hence, it is clear that **the main tenet of socialism, community of goods, must be utterly rejected**, since it only injures those whom it would seem meant to benefit, is directly contrary to the natural rights of mankind, and would introduce confusion and disorder into the commonweal."*

Moreover, this encyclical also addresses the right to own

private property. In it, Pope Leo states: *"... every man has by nature the right to possess property as his own."* Therefore, the right to own property is a precondition for the benefit of the individual and the family.

The following passage from the encyclical makes it clear that the earth is to continually provide for the flourishing of man, and it is on this principle that I believe it is a moral imperative to continue harnessing energy and materials from the earth's fossil fuels to help lift billions of people around the world out of poverty, so that they too can realize the benefits that we take for granted in the West.

According to the Pope's statement below, the State should not interfere, and it should allow the free market to harness the energy that it needs from the earth to increase productivity for the benefit of as many people as possible. The statement clearly points to nature providing a stable source of supplies without any need for the State to intervene:

> *"... man not only should possess the fruits of the earth, but also the very soil, inasmuch as from the produce of the earth he has to lay by provision for the future. Man's needs do not die out, but forever recur; although satisfied today, they demand fresh supplies for tomorrow. Nature accordingly must have given to man a source that is stable and remaining always with him, from which he might look to draw continual supplies. And this stable condition of things he finds solely in the earth and its fruits. There is no need to bring in the State. Man precedes the State, and possesses, prior to the formation of any State, the right of providing for the substance of his body."*

It is important to note that the current pope, Pope Francis, has taken a different stance on fossil fuels, which is contradictory (typical of this pope). He is of the opinion that the fossil fuel industry is doing harm to the environment, and that: *"There is an urgent need to develop policies so that, in the next few years, the emission of carbon dioxide and other highly polluting gases can be drastically reduced, for example, substituting for fossil fuels and developing sources of renewable energy."*

Yet, in the same breath he states that: *"Fresh drinking water is an issue of primary importance, since it is indispensable for human life and for supporting terrestrial and aquatic ecosystems. Sources of fresh water are necessary for health care, agriculture and industry."*[124]

On the surface, these statements may seem reasonable, however, there is some cognitive dissonance going on in my view. The developing world depends on low cost fossil fuels in order to make progress. The best way to produce fresh drinking water is to build and operate water filtration plants. These plants need the energy from fossil fuels to operate. We need to think about the less fortunate in poor nations, and encourage the use of fossil fuels to make progress and improve living conditions.

I disagree with Pope Francis. Rather than vilifying the use of fossil fuels, he should be encouraging poor and developing nations to make use of whatever means necessary to alleviate suffering. This includes using fossil fuels to build the necessary infrastructure to support the health-care and agriculture industries. In my view, Pope Francis got it wrong, but Pope Leo XIII got it right.

Imagine what bitcoin could do for poor and developing countries. These countries have a great opportunity to convert their natural resources directly into bitcoin. In other words, they could start mining their own money! By mining their own bitcoin, they would be able to make more investments in the infrastructure needed to alleviate poverty, improve health care, increase food production, and provide the basic necessities that all we take for granted in the West. Asking the world to use less fossil fuels is nothing more than virtue signaling.

Chapter 8: Why Invest in Bitcoin?

Risk and Cryptocurrency Regulation

Why take risks in life? What really is risk? Most people intuitively know that taking or not taking certain actions may be accompanied with some risk. If I choose to cross the street without looking both ways before crossing, then I could get struck by a moving car. This could result in severe injury or even death.

People intuitively evaluate risk in terms of the likelihood that something harmful could happen, and the resulting impact or consequence of the risk materializing. So when we are about to cross the street, we automatically think about the probability of getting hit by a moving vehicle, and so we look both ways to reduce that probability. We also quickly think about the consequences of being hit, and the severity of the injuries or the possible death that could result.

Risk analysts and risk managers often use the following formula to quantify and calculate risk:

Risk = Likelihood x Severity Level

- where likelihood is a probability score on a scale from 1 to 5, such as 1=improbable, 2=remote, 3=occasional, 4=probable, 5=frequent
- where severity level is subjectively graded on a scale from 1 to 4, such as 1=negligible, 2=marginal, 3=critical, 4=catastrophic

Some people often play it safe, which would be analogous to not crossing the street altogether. That would be the surest way of not getting struck by a moving vehicle, but it also means giving up on the objective of reaching the other side. If risks are not taken, then we simply won't reach our goals.

Fear can be a good thing when it guards us from taking unnecessary risks, however, fear can also be detrimental if it disables us from taking any action at all. Fear can disable a person to the point where life becomes filled with lost opportunities and regret. We have all been afraid of something at some point in our lives, and we know that fear is often the result of ignorance or not having experienced something before.

A good way to overcome fear then, is to educate oneself, and to experience things first hand. These are some common phrases I have used to encourage my children to take risks:

- "face your fear",
- "the only thing we have to fear is fear itself"[125],
- "no risk, no reward", or
- "no pain, no gain."

Taking calculated risks is a part of life, and it also applies to investing. Some people may be overly risk averse when it comes to investing their money, just like the third servant in the parable of the talents who buried his talent and did nothing with it.

Some people may have a lot of money saved in the bank, but they are too afraid to invest it if they are not educated or experienced in financial matters. Most financial experts would agree that holding too much cash is a poor financial decision because cash declines in value over time. For this reason, it is better to purchase or invest in assets with the expectation that assets will increase in value over time.

There are various kinds of assets today that people can invest in, from collectibles such as postage stamps, hockey cards, and wrist watches to financial instruments such as foreign exchange, securities (stocks), and debt-based instruments (bonds). Some investors invest in funds that directly track the S&P 500 Index, which is a prominent index of 500 leading publicly traded companies in the US. These companies are typically sorted into 11 sectors and 24 industry groups. The 11 sectors are: Information Technology, Health Care, Financials, Consumer Discretionary, Communication Services, Industrials, Consumer Staples, Energy, Utilities, Real Estate, and Materials.[126] As mentioned earlier, digital assets and cryptocurrencies could become the 12th sector of the economy one day[127].

Bitcoin and ethereum are the dominant digital assets today, and they are on the cusp of being included as investments for large financial institutions and pension funds. This could result in trillions of dollars entering the space. The high demand for bitcoin and ethereum will likely lead to higher prices of these commodities.

Some investors believe that there is a golden opportunity to invest in bitcoin and ethereum because the US Congress will be voting on a bipartisan bill to introduce comprehensive legislation for the regulation of digital assets. The bill, called the *Responsible Financial Innovation Act*[128], is being proposed by Wyoming Senator Cynthia Lummis and New York Senator Kirsten Gillibrand.

If the bill passes, then this new legislation is expected to address taxation issues, stable coin security, definitions and classifications of digital assets, and much more. This will create a safer environment and mitigate risks for for cryptocurrency investors.

When sufficient cryptocurrency regulations are in place, financial institutions are expected to deploy trillions of dollars into the cryptocurrency industry. For example, as of August 2022, the US-based multi-national investment company, BlackRock (with $10 trillion dollars worth of assets under management), has partnered with Coinbase (the largest American publicly traded cryptocurrency exchange platform) to provide access to cryptocurrency investing for their institutional clients.

I am not a financial advisor, and I have no intention of providing financial advice in this book, but after spending three years studying digital assets, I have been able to reduce my own fear and ignorance about cryptocurrencies to the point where I think the risk of investing in bitcoin is very low, regardless of the ongoing short-term price volatility. I have a long-term view, and I think bitcoin is one of those assets that can be kept for decades, similar to real estate.

Taking the time to properly study bitcoin has enabled me to increase my risk tolerance to the point where I have been able to cross the street. Now that I have arrived on the other side, I am excited about what the future may hold. Only time will tell.

Freedom and Time in the Future

One way to describe freedom is to not be enslaved by others or even by one's own passions. Freedom, therefore, is to exist in a way that allows a person to speak freely, and voluntarily interact or transact with whomever they choose within the bounds of the law. Having the liberty to live your own life according to your own decisions and based on your own free will, while respecting the rule of law, is one way to describe freedom.

In my personal case, I found freedom by recognizing that I was a slave to a life caught up in a world of lies, e.g., a secular, left-wing, Hollywood culture. When I turned my back on that life and looked towards beauty, truth, and goodness, it was ultimately Christ that freed me from my sins and gave me my freedom back.

"For freedom Christ has set us free; stand fast therefore, and do not submit again to a yoke of slavery."[129]

In a way, I experienced freedom when the scales fell from my eyes, just as Saul experienced after being healed. From the New Testament, we learn that Saul was struck by blindness for three days while approaching Damascus, and then later the scales fell from his eyes after being healed by Jesus through Anani'as:

> *"So Anani'as departed and entered the house. And laying hands on him he said, 'Brother Saul, the Lord Jesus who appeared to you on the road by which you came, has sent me that you may regain your sight and be filled with the Holy Spirit.' And immediately something like scales fell from his eyes and he regained his sight. Then he rose and was baptized, and took food and was strengthened."[130]*

When Saul regained his sight, it triggered a life-changing transformation in him. He stopped persecuting the Jews, and instead he began proclaiming that Jesus was the Son of God. Ironically, the Jews then sought to kill Saul because they didn't like what he was saying about Jesus.

Jesus's disciples were able to intervene, and they brought Saul to the apostles. After Saul's conversion, he changed his name to Paul, the Latin version of his name. As Paul, he voluntarily chose to become a missionary preacher to the Gentiles, and he thought of himself as being *"free from all men."*[131]

Another aspect of freedom, apart from not being a slave or oppressed by others, is to have an abundance of time to spend as you see fit. Having the time to do the things you truly want to do in life usually requires financial freedom, or at least a big bank account.

Most people end up spending the majority of their time working to earn a living, with only a few days of the year as holidays in the form of paid vacation days. These vacation days provide employees with more time to rest and to enjoy leisure activities. The wealthier and more financially secure a person is, in general, the more free time they have to do whatever they wish.

The old adage, money buys time, is in some sense quite true. Of course time is not something that can be created or destroyed, so we can't literally buy it, but we do have control over how we choose to spend it. Time can be thought of as being a scarce resource, one that can never be replenished, but something to use, hopefully doing something productive, while we are still alive.

If bitcoin truly is the best money available, and if the world adopts it as a world reserve asset, then I believe bitcoin will be capable of buying more time than any other government-issued currency.

Most people, out of necessity, are required to work at a job for several hours per day for five or more days per week, in order to earn enough money to sustain their material lives. When the amount of money a person possesses significantly exceeds what they need, then they can spend their time doing other things. Having true freedom means having the ability to spend your time doing the things you really want to do. I believe that owning bitcoin is the best way to increase wealth, which can then buy more time.

In hunter and gatherer societies, a lot of time was spent on finding and preparing food to survive. More sophisticated tools were eventually made to make hunting and gathering more efficient, which freed up time to do other things. When humans formed agricultural societies, only a few people relative to the human population needed to take care of food production, which enabled the rest of the population to have more time to specialize in doing other kinds of work.

Human ingenuity and the inventive process accelerated to such a degree that it drastically changed how we live today. Our productivity has enabled us to trade goods and services with other nations, resulting in an increase in living standards for the masses. This was all enabled by the industrial revolution.

During the industrial revolution, work became hyperspecialized, which enabled more people to participate in the economy and to increase their wealth. It also gave the intellectuals in society more time to think and write, thereby spreading knowledge throughout the population. Volumes of information and knowledge could then be stored in books, thanks to Johannes Gutenberg's invention of the printing press.

There is no doubt that the industrial revolution enabled people to invent new gadgets and new technologies, especially new forms of transportation such as trains, planes and automobiles. These new forms of transportation enabled greater movement around the world, and it began to connect us physically together through travel and trade between countries. It contributed to increasing wealth all around the world.

Today, technological advancements continue to make things more efficient, as we have surpassed the industrial revolution and entered into the information age. We can now use computing, the internet, wireless communications, e-commerce, and now the blockchain to transmit monetary value to each other.

Given all of these advancements, it is no wonder why many people are choosing to spend more of their time online to educate themselves, communicate with each other, and participate in online communities through social media. The television and movie industry, and now gaming are all largely conducted online. The lines between the physical world and the online world are blurring with new advancements in virtual reality, the metaverse, and artificial intelligence.

The next logical transition will be the pervasiveness of robots or robotic agents in serving humans. I can imagine a world where humans will interact and transact with robots, and robots will interact and transact with each other using bitcoin.

For example, in the not too distant future, I can imagine paying a robot to do my chores. I could hire a robot to clear the snow off my driveway during the winter, or mow my lawn in the summer.

The robot could be hailed like a taxi, and it would just show up at my house, do the job, and then leave. There would be no need for me to purchase and store robotic gadgets in my home.

The integration of robots to assist humans could operate on a pay-as-you-go model. For example, if I run out of cream for my coffee, I could hail a robot, which would arrive in a driverless taxi (arranged by the robot of course), and the robot would ring my doorbell to hand me my cream. All of this would be possible in real time by paying the robot in bitcoin (in advance or upon delivery).

Fiat Money Erodes Time

Today's government-issued fiat currencies are a terrible store of value. The wealth of many nations continues to decline, especially in nations with hyperinflating fiat currencies. The end result is that fewer people have the means to purchase a home anymore, and the cost of goods and services continues to increase to the point where everything keeps getting more expensive. Rising costs are not only a reflection of simple supply and demand forces, but rather the interference of governments in corrupting and inflating the world's fiat currencies.

Fiat money is a weak form of money because it devalues over time. This means that when we work to earn money today, the fiat money earned doesn't go as far as it used to. As a result, people need to work longer hours, living paycheck to paycheck, just to make ends meet. This means less free time.

Fiat money prevents people from achieving wealth because it is literally a bad form of money. It just doesn't retain enough value to buy the free time that most people desire. When fiat money loses its purchasing power over time, as it has been over the past several decades, people end up poorer. Many of us find ourselves in a rat race, spinning our wheels, unable to get ahead.

This phenomenon has clearly impacted the family structure, requiring two parents to work, leaving children to raise themselves, or in some cases to be raised by nannies. Parents just don't have the time anymore to raise their own children, which is likely a contributing factor to the increase in many societal ills.

As discussed earlier in this book, the answer to accumulating wealth and freedom lies in owning assets because assets are a better store of value than holding cash. The problem, however, is that only a small percentage of people in the world can own assets. For example, to be able to purchase a home today, most people need to take on large mortgage loan, and they end up remaining in debt for the majority of their lives.

For this reason, homeowners today are not really owners, they are debtors. Because they are debtors, they don't truly own their home, the bank does. The home should only be considered their asset once the mortgage loan has been fully paid. Anything purchased using the bank's money is really the bank's asset until you have paid off the loan.

The fact is, most of us are running on a hamster wheel, and we are getting nowhere. The reason has to do with the fact that the fiat money we earn continues to be debased at an alarming rate. Imagine if wages and salaries were paid in gold rather than dollars. Wouldn't that be better?

The only problem with getting paid in gold is that there isn't enough gold in the world to go around, and even if there was, it would not be practical as a medium of exchange. Gold is just too heavy and not that portable.

It is easier for governments to just print fiat money into existence, but as mentioned many times now, fiat money is bad money. Here are some example scenarios showing how bad money effectively failed the citizens of these nations due to rampant hyperinflation[132]:

- In 1923 Germany's Papiermark experienced 325,000,000% inflation, and was replaced by the Rentenmark. Hyperinflation enabled Adolf Hitler to gain power[133].

- In 1926 the Austrian Pengo replaced the Austrian-Hungarian Korona, and by 1946 the highest Pengo note was 100,000,000,000,000,000. This Pengo was then replaced by the Forint in the 1960s.

- Between 1971 and 1981 in Chile, their central bank printed their unbacked currency, Escudo, at an alarming rate which resulted in an inflation rate of 1200% by the end of 1973. The Escudo was then replaced by the New Peso at a rate of 1000 to 1. Argentina and Peru also experienced something similar in the 1980s and 1990s.

- Due to civil war in Angola, its currency, the Kwanza, hyperinflated to a 500,000 banknote by 1995, which had to replaced by a New Kwanza.

- Between 1988 and 1989 the Yugoslavian Dinar had 2,000,000 notes, which were replaced by the New Dinar in 1992, and by 1994 inflation was increasing at a rate of 100% per day.

- After the Cold War many Eastern Bloc states began to experience the pains of currency inflation, such as Belarus. It had a 5,000,000 note and so the currency was replaced by the new Ruble at an exchange rate of 1 to 1000. Presently, the highest denomination is the 100,000,000 Ruble.

- In Zimbabwe their currency inflated to 1730% by 2006, and then by mid 2007 it reached a yearly increase of 11,000%. By May 2008, 100 Million and 250 Million New Zimbabwe Dollars (ZWD) denominated notes were released, and two weeks later a 500 Million ZWD note was introduced, valued at about USD $2.50. A 100 Billion ZWD was released in 2008, and by August 2008 the government removed ten zeros from the currency, and 10 Billion ZWD became equal to 1 New ZWD.

- As of May 2022 the Lebanese pound (LPD) had an annual

inflation rate of 211%, an increase from the previous month's annual inflation rate of 206%[134]. The highest bank notes are denominated in 100,000 Pounds. More than 70% of the Lebanese people live under the poverty line, and the majority are unable to secure basic needs.

Given today's geopolitical climate, there are some who believe that the US dollar is on its way to collapse by the end of this decade. Legendary investor and billionaire Stanley Druckenmiller said that he does not expect the US dollar to remain the world's leading reserve asset within 15 years[135]. He also believes that bitcoin is better than gold.

Widespread Bitcoin Adoption Coming Soon

Given the weakness of fiat currencies, it is clear to me that bitcoin's superior monetary properties will serve to better preserve monetary value over time. Its supply cannot be manipulated by governments, and therefore it will never suffer from inflation.

The fact that the bitcoin monetary system was designed with a hard-cap of 21 million bitcoin, and that approximately 1.5 million bitcoin are remaining to be mined by the year 2140, means that bitcoin is best positioned to become a world reserve asset. If bitcoin attains the status of a world reserve asset, then this will help countries around the world to solve their inflation problems. It may even reduce poverty and corruption in those countries because bitcoin can't be controlled or manipulated, and I am convinced that it will always hold its value over time, similar to gold.

For the wealthier nations, bitcoin will be a desirable method of receiving wages and paying for goods and services due to its anti-inflationary properties. This will enable people to buy more time, and therefore more freedom. In fact, some professional athletes and politicians have already chosen to receive some of their salary in bitcoin[136].

As of September 2022, many countries have adopted cryptocurrencies. The top 20 countries in the world that use cryptocurrencies are ranked as follows: Vietnam, Philippines, Ukraine, India, United States, Pakistan, Brazil, Thailand, Russia, China, Nigeria, Turkey, Argentina, Morocco, Colombia, Nepal, United Kingdom, Ecuador, Kenya, Indonesia.[137]

As fiat currencies continue to collapse around the world, the case for bitcoin becomes more obvious. A bank is only needed to store and transact in fiat currency, but with bitcoin, anyone with a device connected to the internet can store, send and receive bitcoin, effectively being their own bank.

In the digital assets space, a bank is obsolete. Cryptocurrencies and digital assets such as bitcoin remain safe and secure on the blockchain. The trust is in the blockchain's software code rather than in people.

In this way, individuals become their own bank by holding and controlling the private keys, similar to holding the keys to your own safety deposit box. A commonly held expression in the cryptocurrency community is *"not your keys, not your coin"*. The world can truly become bankless and all individuals can transact with each other in a seamless peer-to-peer manner without government manipulation of the currency.

As more people become educated and familiar with cryptocurrency, bitcoin adoption is expected to increase exponentially. In its first 10 years, bitcoin has seen a much faster adoption rate than the internet. *"By 2019, the number of Bitcoin users had reached 35 million, which is more than double the number of users the internet had in its first 10 years ... The number of Bitcoin users has grown by more than 150%, compared to just 30% growth for the internet over the same period."*[138]

A 2018 study examined Metcalfe's Law as a model for bitcoin's value. The results of the study concluded that bitcoin's price, in the medium- to long-term, appears to follow Metcalfe's law[139]. The mathematics of Metcalfe's Law is described in the same paper as follows:

> *"Metcalfe's law is based on the mathematical tautology describing connectivity among n users. As more people join a network, they add to the value of the network nonlinearly; i.e., the value of the network is proportional to the square of the number of users."*

If the Metcalfe model accurately describes bitcoin's value from network effects, then there is potential for significant value yet to be gained from the bitcoin network. Some would say that it is still very early to invest in bitcoin, similar to the mid-1990s, when the general population began to adopt the internet to transmit and consume information via a web browser.

While most people may find it technically challenging to acquire bitcoin because of the need to purchase it from a cryptocurrency exchange and managing and storing private keys, another option is to invest in a spot bitcoin ETF. This will avoid all of the technical matters and the need to manage the storage of private keys. ETFs are expected to enable large institutional investors to onboard their clients to bitcoin investing.

In Canada, several approved spot bitcoin ETFs were launched in 2021. In the US, billions of dollars of investment capital are now expected to flow into spot bitcoin ETFs beginning in January 2024. These inflows into bitcoin will create a demand shock, which is expected to further increase bitcoin's value as an asset.

I think it is time for the Catholic Church to consider adopting bitcoin or investing in a spot bitcoin ETF. Bitcoin can help the Church to save and grow its funds to enable good works and helping the poor in their communities.

Local parishes, including priests, can discern how to invest in a morally permissible way that is aligned with the faith. Catholics should read, *Mensuram Bonam*[140], a 46-page document that outlines "faith-based measures for Catholic investors", and explains how to determine whether or not your investments are in keeping with guidance from the Vatican's *Pontifical Academy of Social Sciences*. After reading the document myself, I have concluded that investing in bitcoin is indeed ethically and morally aligned with Catholic social teaching.

Priests should consider investing a small portion of their donations, say 5%, into bitcoin or a spot bitcoin ETF. The investment can then be included on the parish balance sheet, and transparent to the parish community. As bitcoin appreciates in value over 5 to 10 years, some of it can be sold to help pay for operations and maintenance expenses, such as an expensive roof replacement or to help fundraising initiatives within the parish community and secular surrounding communities. I believe that a medium- to long-term investment in bitcoin can benefit the Church significantly, thereby helping it to build the Kingdom of God.

A New Paradigm with Bitcoin

It is hard for people to imagine how a world without government-issued fiat currencies could function. Governments around the world have issued fiat currencies for centuries, and inflation has always been an accepted feature, even though we know that it always devalues over time and never appreciates. The purchasing power always decreases, and the prices of goods and services always increase.

Governments continue to use the failing ideology of Keynesian economics to justify their money printing practices, believing that increasing the money supply is necessary to support a growing economy. The time has come to jettison Keynesian economics, and adopt Austrian economics and bitcoin. [141]

But how can an economy function with bitcoin? How would

bitcoin's anti-inflationary or deflationary currency actually support a growing economy? Isn't inflation necessary to support a growing population?

The answer is quite simple if you recognize that our current fiat currency system is not based on any magical formula for determining the appropriate supply of money that needs to exist in the economic system. We have already seen countries around the world with varying money supplies, varying interest rates, and with varying populations, and not a single government really knows what amount of money is needed for the population to thrive. Government officials and academia have been conditioned to accept Keynesian economics as the only system we have, but this is not the case.

Rather than living in an inflationary environment, it is possible to conceive of living in a deflationary one. Keynesians would argue that deflation will destroy demand, but this is not true. We know this is not true because it has already been observed in the consumer electronics industry.

Despite the decline in prices of televisions, phone, and computers over the last 30 years, the quality of these products continues to increase. Regardless of declining prices, consumers across the globe continue to make purchases. Therefore, bitcoin's deflationary pressure would not negatively impact demand for goods within society.

With bitcoin, an entirely new paradigm is possible. Bitcoin has a fixed supply of 21 million, and the last bitcoin to be mined will occur in the year 2140. After that, no more bitcoin will be mined, and the bitcoin core software protocol will prevent any attempt to expand the bitcoin supply.

By the year 2140, I think it is quite probable that the prices for goods and services will be denominated in bitcoin. Employers will pay employee salaries and wages in bitcoin.

As more and more people populate the earth, the amount of

bitcoin will never run out because of the divisibility of bitcoin, which is far more divisible than fiat currencies. One bitcoin can be divided into 8 decimal places, with constituent units called, *satoshis* (SATS). For example, 1 BTC = 100 million SATS. Online conversion tools can be used to convert SATS to USD and vice versa. For example, USD $1 = 3,826 SATS or 0.000038 BTC on August 21, 2023.

In a world without inflation, and one where the currency can no longer be depreciated in value but only appreciate, an appreciating currency would mean higher purchasing power. In other words, if a loaf of bread were to cost 3,826 SATS today, then the price would be lower in the future because of the appreciation of the value of bitcoin. That same loaf of bread may only cost 3,500 SATS instead of 3,826 SATS in the future.

This would mean that goods and services would appear to get cheaper, but what it really means is that the purchasing power of the currency has become stronger. This is hard to imagine, but it would work under the principles of Austrian economics. It is an entirely different paradigm from what we are experiencing today. Imagine earning and storing your hard-earned money in an appreciating currency rather than a depreciating currency.

No government or financial institution can manipulate the bitcoin monetary system because it uses military-grade cryptography to produce a decentralized ledger, which holds the final truth of all peer-to-peer bitcoin transactions. This eliminates the need for a bank to store and manage money.

Governments around the world are realizing that bitcoin is the best money available, and they see the writing on the wall. It is likely that people and economies will gradually reduce their reliance on US dollars and other fiat currencies in favour of bitcoin. Bitcoin is money of the people, and it allows every individual in the world, having a cell phone with access to the internet, to store monetary value and participate in the economy.

Chapter 9: Two Sets of Ten Commandments

An Open Heart and Mind

Two thousand years ago, the Angel Gabriel announced to the Blessed Virgin Mary that the Holy Spirit would overshadow her and she would give birth to a child who was to be named, Jesus. Nine months later, Jesus Christ was born.

When Jesus was in his 30s, he revealed himself to be the Messiah, the incarnation of God himself. His purpose was to enter his own creation to teach us how to be his disciple, and then he redeemed us by saving us from our sins through his death and resurrection.

About fifteen years ago, I believe that God used Satoshi Nakamoto (anonymous) as his instrument to invent bitcoin. Satoshi released bitcoin onto the internet to save us from a broken financial world during the 2008 financial crisis. Bitcoin now offers every individual the ability to own a valuable digital asset, functioning as a superior store of value for all 8 billion people in the world. Although it is possible to live a life without Jesus and without bitcoin, I believe that people can become both spiritually and financially richer if they open their hearts and minds to both.

The Judeo-Christian value system, which gave rise to the West, is built on the moral foundation of the Ten Commandments. While the Ten Commandments may be too difficult for some to live by, the bar is set high for good reason. Christians believe that these commandments are necessary in order to live a virtuous life, worthy of God.

Bitcoin operates according to a set of unbreakable rules written into code, such that it has created a new kind of monetary system to live by. It does away with the scourge of government-issued fiat currencies and banks, and provides an alternative peer-to-peer monetary system where the individual effectively becomes their own bank. This can help over one billion people in the world, who are currently bankless or underbanked, to be included in the economy.

As already described, a world operating on bitcoin may help people to aspire to live in accordance with the first two servants in Jesus' Parable of the Talents. These two servants made more than they were given, and they gladly gave it all back to their master. For me, this would be similar to attaining wealth, and then participating in philanthropy.

Regardless of your thoughts about God, the Judeo-Christian moral value system and its Ten Commandments are the foundation for Western civilization.

I have introduced another set of Ten Commandments, not to replace God's Ten Commandments, but to expand upon the Parable of the Talents with the hope of attaining financial freedom. Regardless of what you think about bitcoin, I sincerely hope that you will keep an open mind while reading my Ten Commandments for Financial Freedom. For me, both sets of ten commandments help me to strive to become the best version of myself.

The Ten Commandments

Below are The Ten Commandments accompanied with an examination of conscience taken from the Archdiocese of Toronto website[142]. As a practicing Catholic, although I know I fall short, I am still striving to live by them as best I can.

1. I am the Lord your God: you shall not have strange Gods before me.

Have I treated people, events, or things as more important than

God?

2. You shall not take the name of the Lord your God in vain.
Have my words, actively or passively, put down God, His Church, or His people?

3. Remember to keep holy the Lord's Day.
Do I go to Mass every Sunday (or Saturday Vigil) and on Holy Days of Obligation (Jan. 1; Dec. 25)? Do I avoid, when possible, work that impedes worship to God, joy for the Lord's Day, and proper relaxation of mind and body? Do I look for ways to spend time with family or in service on Sunday?

4. Honor your father and your mother.
Do I show my parents or elders due respect? Do I seek to maintain good communication with them where possible? Do I criticize them for lacking skills I think they should have?

5. You shall not kill.
Have I harmed another through physical, verbal, or emotional means, including gossip or manipulation of any kind?

6. You shall not commit adultery.
Have I respected the physical and sexual dignity of others and of myself?

7. You shall not steal.
Have I taken things that belong to others; have I taken credit that belongs to others; have I wasted the time of others?

8. You shall not bear false witness against your neighbour.
Have I gossiped, told lies, or embellished stories at the expense of another?

9. You shall not covet your neighbour's spouse.
Have I honored my spouse with my full affection and exclusive love?

10. You shall not covet your neighbour's goods.
Am I content with my own means and needs, or do I compare myself to others unnecessarily?

The Ten Commandments for Financial Freedom

These are my Ten Commandments along with my personal notes for the hope of achieving financial freedom.

1. Live in a country that respects private property rights, foundational to freedom itself.

Do I understand that property does not really mean land, but it refers to ownership? Any object that is owned is property, and it inherently excludes others from having the right to own or use that same object. Throughout common law history, people have had the right to acquire, use, and dispose of property freely. Not only does this allow for freedom, but it allows citizens of a nation to own private property for their own productive use, and to trade the fruits of their labour with others, which increases the overall wealth of a society. Without private property rights, nations end up being poorer.

2. Encourage decentralization over centralization.

Have I studied the harm caused by Marxism, communism, and socialism? Have I studied the differences between

Austrian and Keynesian economics? Do I understand the benefits of decentralization and true free-market capitalism over central planning? Do I acknowledge that if we truly had free-market capitalism, then it would achieve optimum capital allocation, production, price signals, and adaptation to the forces of supply and demand? Have I pondered the natural phenomenon and beauty of murmurations? Do I respect the freedom of others to make their own decisions given the information at hand? To put it simply, decentralization is better for human flourishing. Countries with strong centralization and control tend to become dictatorships, detrimental to its citizens.

3. Become financially literate.

Do I recognize the difference between government-issued fiat currencies, physical assets, and digital assets such as bitcoin? Have I studied the history of money, and do I truly understand how governments manipulate the money supply and interest rates to cause inflation and debasement of currencies, effectively making us all poorer over time?

4. Serve your fellow man.

Have I studied what it means to have a vocation? Have I thought about the four different ways to earn a just living? Rather than remaining an employee my entire life, have I considered taking on more risk by starting a business or becoming self-employed? Do I understand that taking risks and investing in assets are important? Do I have an entrepreneurial spirit, and do I recognize that businesses are good because they provide employment and a livelihood to others? Whatever kind of work that I do, do I pay attention to the details and do my work as best I can? *"You, therefore, must be perfect, as your heavenly Father is perfect."* -- Matthew 5:48.

5. Purchase, accumulate, and hold assets for many years.

Have I taken the time to study various asset classes, and have I purchased any for the benefit of myself and my descendants? Do I recognize that it is never too late to purchase an asset, even if it seems to have appreciated too much already? Do I understand that a home purchased with a mortgage to live in is not an asset, but a liability? Have I studied historical values of various assets over time to determine if they have outpaced inflation? Do I adopt a long-term investment horizon of ten or more years? The price of one bitcoin has appreciated immensely since its inception. In February 2011 it surpassed $1, by the end of 2012 it surpassed $10, by 2013 it surpassed $100, by 2014 it surpassed $1000, and by 2017 it surpassed $10,000. Is it possible for bitcoin to surpass $100,000 some day?

6. Respect the need for energy consumption to get work done.

Have I studied the physics of energy and work, and do I respect that without energy, civilizations would not make progress? Do I recognize that countries with natural resources and advanced technologies tend to be wealthier and more secure than countries without natural resources and without technology? Just as energy is needed to operate the machines that help to build all of the physical infrastructure around us, so too is energy needed to operate computers for the purpose of building and securing bitcoin. Bitcoin's intrinsic value comes from the fact that it relies on energy and a proof-of-work mechanism to create a revolutionary technology and monetary system. Expending energy to create bitcoin is a feature, not a bug.

7. You shall not be dependent on others for your financial

needs (adults only).

Do I have a sense of entitlement, and do I depend on the government to take care of me? Do I recognize that, apart from mental illness or for health reasons, I should not depend on the government or on others for my welfare? As an exception, spouses can and should depend on each other, for better or for worse, for richer or for poorer, in sickness and in health, to love and to cherish, till death do them part.

8. You shall not love money for the love of money is the root of all evil.

Money itself is not evil. It is just a technology than can be used for good or for evil purposes. There is nothing wrong with wanting to be rich and to obtain wealth as long as you use your wealth responsibly and not selfishly. Using your wealth to promote a good cause for the benefit of others is righteous. Be like the first two servants in Jesus' Parable of the Talents who doubled their talents and gave it to their master. Am I able to give more than I have received, or do I love money so much that I have elevated it to an idol for my own selfish pleasures above God and others? If I love money in this way, then it is evil.

9. You shall not save cash because cash is trash.

Do I recognize the problem of inflation and hyperinflation? Governments around the world have been reckless in debasing fiat currencies and destroying their purchasing power. Even in wealthy nations, currencies have decreased in value slowly but significantly over the past few decades. Fiat currencies are not backed by precious metals anymore, and so they lose their value over time. Rather than saving cash, it is better to convert the cash into assets that retain or appreciate in value over time.

10. You shall not succumb to instant gratification.

Do I succumb to instant gratification, or do I have the patience to delay gratification in anticipation for something better in the future? Do I take on a lot of debt in order to be able to have the latest and greatest material goods, just to keep up with the Jones'? Am I able to lower my time preference (wait) and live within my own means? Do I spend my money immediately to purchase unnecessary things, or do I save to purchase assets that may increase in value over time?

Where Does Your Treasure Lie?

Earthly Treasure

After studying bitcoin, I now fully comprehend what it is, and I am aware of its implications on individuals, families, businesses, governments, and the Church. Believers in bitcoin greatly respect Satoshi Nakamoto because he invented the hardest money ever known, which many believe has the status of digital gold.

It is my hope that more people will educate themselves about bitcoin, possibly the greatest earthly treasure known to man. Bitcoin is the antidote to the broken traditional financial system in our world, and it is the opposite of government-controlled fiat currency. Having an open and curious mind helped me to start my own journey in understanding bitcoin, and now that I understand it, I have hope for financial freedom and self sovereignty.

Heavenly Treasure

The *Three Parables* below, taken from the Gospel of Matthew, describe how driven a person can be in order to find and obtain an earthly treasure. It reveals to what great lengths we are willing to go to obtain it. The parables also reveal that the kingdom of heaven will be like a treasure. It sounds wonderful, and I truly believe that it is real. I know that I can't save myself or earn my way into heaven, but I know that God is merciful and just, and that my eternal salvation is entirely in his hands. This wisdom has helped me to put earthly treasures such as bitcoin into their proper context:

Three Parables

"The kingdom of heaven is like treasure hidden in a field, which a man found and covered up; then in his joy he goes and sells all that he has and buys that field.

"Again, the kingdom of heaven is like a merchant in search of fine pearls, who, on finding one pearl of great value, went and sold all that he had and bought it.

"Again, the kingdom of heaven is like a net which was thrown into the sea and gathered fish of every kind; when it was full, men drew it ashore and sat down and sorted the good into vessels but threw away the bad. So it will be at the close of the age. The angels will come out and separate the evil from the righteous, and throw them into the furnace of fire; there men will weep and gnash their teeth.

In Catholicism, the Blessed Virgin Mary, also known as the Immaculate Conception, is revered because God made her perfect and stainless so that she could be the vessel through which God chose to enter his creation as Jesus Christ. I put all of my hope and trust in Jesus. While earthly treasures such as bitcoin are good, maybe even perfect according to earthly standards, they are still passing and fleeting.

The ultimate treasure is eternal life in heaven. For this reason, I have to remind myself *"to stay focused on things that are above, not on things that are on earth."*[143]

"Do not lay up for yourselves treasures on earth, where moth and rust consume and where thieves break in and steal, but lay up for yourselves treasures in heaven, where neither moth nor rust consumes and where thieves do not break in and steal. For where your treasure is, there will your heart be also."[144]

Acknowledgments

I am grateful to several priests in Ottawa, Canada, who continue to unpack the Gospel and share their wisdom at Sunday Mass.

It is impossible to list everyone who helped me to understand and appreciate bitcoin, but I wish to thank some online influencers, such as Robert Breedlove, Michael Saylor, Natalie Brunell, Jason Lowery, Greg Foss, Andreas Antonopoulos, Anthony Pompliano, Lyn Alden, David Lin, Dylan LeClair, Nik Bhatia, Balaji Srinivasan, Raoul Pal (Real Vision), George Tung (Cryptos R Us), James Mullarney (Invest Answers), Sam (My Financial Friend), British Hodl, and Max Keiser. It has truly been edifying and entertaining to listen to them.

I am also grateful to authors such as Saifedean Ammous and Jeff Booth who have written books about bitcoin, Austrian economics, and deflation[145].

I would especially like to thank Paul Malvern and Tim McCauley for their suggestions and encouragement, and my wife and children for putting up with my constant enthusiasm for bitcoin.

Last but not least, I would like to thank OpenAI for releasing the free creative image generator, DALL-E, which automatically generated the image on the front cover of this book.

About the Author

Jasbir Singh is a federal pubic servant working in the field of data science to gather business intelligence. He is a second-generation Canadian born of Sikh Indian parents who immigrated to Canada in the late 1960s.

He was raised and educated in Ottawa, and after graduating from university with bachelor's degrees in biotechnology and education, he moved to Osaka and Tokyo, Japan during the mid 1990s to work as a high school math and science teacher for several years.

When Jasbir moved back home to Canada in the late 1990s, he caught the high-tech bug, and decided to complete another undergraduate degree in software engineering. At the same time, he took up day trading as a hobby with the money that he earned in Japan.

After experiencing the roller-coaster boom and bust of the dot-com bubble in March 2000, he later experienced an existential crisis. This eventually led to his conversion to Catholicism in 2003.

In 2021, after recognizing the beauty, truth, and goodness of bitcoin, Jasbir set out on a new mission to educate his family and friends about bitcoin. This book is his first attempt. He has aspirations to change careers one day to contribute to the Web 3.0 economy.

Jasbir celebrates weekly Mass at a local parish, participates in faith and fellowship events, such as *That Man Is You,* and he is a member of the Knights of Columbus. He lives with his wife and children in Ottawa, Canada.

Follow Jasbir on X @ViewBitcoin.

1. Mann, Ashi. Master of Arts Thesis - Investigating Factors Related to Fear, Uncertainty, and Doubt (FUD) in End-User Cryptocurrency Behaviours. Carleton University (August 2023).
2. Kuiper, Chris and Neureuter, Jack. Bitcoin First Revisited – Why investors need to consider bitcoin separately from other digital assets. Fidelity (October 4, 2023).
3. Argentine Presidential candidate: Bitcoin is the natural reaction against the scam of central banking. https://youtu.be/BDwKNLmD4P0 (January 7, 2023).
4. Fieldhouse, Stuart. Crypto traders are planning to front run ETF news, says fund manager. The Armchair Trader (December 6, 2023). Nelson, Rob. With crypto, retail investors have a chance to front-run Wall Street for the first time. The Street Crypto (November 21, 2023).
5. Gospel of Matthew, 22:16-22. https://www.biblegateway.com/passage/?search=matthew+22%3A16-22&version=RSV
6. Svetski, Aleksandar. Fix the Money, Fix the World. Bitcoin Magazine (2021)
7. The Art of Manliness Podcast: Episode #14, 2010, https://www.artofmanliness.com/character/advice/the-art-of-manliness-podcast-episode-14-men-to-boys-and-the-making-of-modern-immaturity/
8. Cross, Gary. Men to Boys: The Making of Modern Immaturity, Columbia University Press, 2008.
9. Starkey, Arun. How Star Trek changed popular culture forever. Far Out (September 8th, 2021).
10. Singh, Jasbir. Canadian Converts – The Path to Rome. pp. 220-240, Justin Press (2009).
11. Woods, Thomas E. How the Catholic Church Built Western Civilization. Ignatius Press, 2013.
12. Kiyosaki, Robert. Rich Dad Poor Dad. Business Plus, New York (2001).
13. Azhari and Bassam. Bank hold ups snowball in Lebanon as depositors demand their own money. Reuters (September 2022).
14. Adams, Michael. Who is Satoshi Nakamoto? Forbes (March 18 2023).
15. Lioudis, Nick. Treasury Bonds vs. Treasury Notes vs. Treasury Bills: What's the Difference? Investopedia (May 24, 2023).
16. St. Paul's Second Letter to the Thessalonians, 2 Thessalonians 3:7-12. https://www.biblegateway.com/passage/?search=2+thessalonians+3%3A7-12&version=RSV
17. Williams, Walter. (2014). Walter Williams on Capitalism. *Foundation for Economic Education*. https://fee.org/articles/walter-williams-at-fee/.
18. Gospel of Matthew, 20:13-15. https://www.biblegateway.com/passage/?search=matthew+20%3A13-15&version=RSV
19. Jeremiah 1:5. https://www.biblegateway.com/passage/?search=Jeremiah%201&version=RSV
20. Gospel of Matthew 22:36-40. https://www.biblegateway.com/passage/?search=matthew+22%3A36-40&version=RSV

21. Escriva, Josemaria. "Friends of God", point 55, 1977, www.escrivaworks.org/book/friends_of_god/point/55
22. Ammous, Saifedean. Principles of Economics. Chapter 2, The Saif House (2023).
23. Gospel of Matthew, 20:13-15. https://www.biblegateway.com/passage/?search=matthew+20%3A13-15&version=RSV
24. Hazlitt, Henry. Economics in One Lesson, Penguin Random House LLC, 1946, 1962, 1979, 1988.
25. Perry, Mark J. Quotation of the Day: Henry Hazlitt on the Minimum Wage. American Enterprise Institute (February 15, 2013).
26. Hazlitt, Henry. Man Versus the Welfare State. Crown Publishing Group (1969).
27. Catechism of the Catholic Church. Part Three, Section One, Chapter Two, Article 1 – The Person and Society (paragraph 1885).
28. Catechism of the Catholic Church. Part Three, Section Two, Chapter Two, Article 7 – The Seventh Commandment, You shall not steal (paragraphs 2431 and 2432).
29. Milei, Javier. Javier Milei addresses World Economic Forum in Davos (full speech). National Post (January 18, 2024).
30. Rand, Ayn. The Fountainhead, Penguin Canada (2008).
31. Rand, Ayn. Atlas Shrugged, Signet (1996).
32. Genders, Rights and Freedom of Speech. Interview with Jordan Peterson on the Agenda with Steve Paikin (2016).
33. Walker, Andrew T. The Gospel and the Natural Law. First Things (December 8, 2020).
34. Hebrews 8:10. https://www.biblegateway.com/passage/?search=hebrews+8%3A10&version=RSV
35. Romans 2. Saint Paul's Letter to the Romans - The Righteous Judgment of God.
36. The Natural Moral Law, Catechism of the Catholic Church #1954 to #1960.
37. Bastiat, Frederic. The Law. Creative Commons (1850 classic).
38. Rothbard, Murray. The Ethics of Liberty. NYU Press, 1998.
39. Lowery, Jason Paul. Softwar: A Novel Theory on Power Projection and the National Strategic Significance of Bitcoin (2023).
40. The Four Social Revolutions. https://socialsci.libretexts.org/Bookshelves/Sociology/Introduction_to_Sociology/Sociology_(Boundless)/21%3A_Social_Change/21.02%3A_Sources_of_Social_Change/21.2C%3A_The_Four_Social_Revolutions
41. Wood, Marilee. Glass beads from pre-European contact sub-Saharan Africa: Peter Francis' work revisited and updated. Archaeological Research in Asia. Volume 6, June 2016.
42. Gospel of Matthew 26: 14-16
43. Gospel of Matthew 27:3-4
44. Bitcoin and the Power Projection Game, The Jason Lowery Series, Episode 1 (WiM124),

https://youtu.be/wRxc7uUqAyE
45. Gorton, David. How Does Money Supply Affect Inflation? Investopedia (August 22, 2023).
46. Federal Reserve Bank of St. Louis – https://fred.stlouisfed.org/series/M1SL
47. Clear, James. 40 Years of Stanford Research Found That People With This One Quality Are More Likely to Succeed.
48. https://www.marketwatch.com/story/founder-of-worlds-largest-hedge-fund-says-cash-is-trash-as-the-dow-soars-to-records-2020-01-21
49. Gospel of Matthew 25:14-30. https://www.biblegateway.com/passage/?search=matthew+25%3A14-30&version=RSV
50. Bishop Robert Barron. The Deeper Meaning of the Parable of the Talents. The Catholic World Report (2014).
51. Wikipedia. https://en.m.wikipedia.org/wiki/Mt._Gox
52. Nakamoto, Satoshi. Bitcoin: A Peer-to-Peer Electronic Cash System (October 31, 2008).
53. Blockchain. https://en.m.wikipedia.org/wiki/Blockchain
54. Maraia, Mark. Bitcoin's Blockchain is the Timechain, Let's Call it That. Bitcoin Magazine (2001).
55. Bitnodes. https://bitnodes.io/dashboard/?days=90
56. Hamdy and Bogosian. Explaining the Bitcoin Block Reward. https://argoblockchain.com//articles/explaining-the-bitcoin-block-reward
57. Staff of the Ontario Securities Commission. QuadrigaCX – A Review by Staff of the Ontario Securities Commission (April 14, 2020).
58. The Saylor Series, Episodes 1 to 9, Robert Breedlove (2021). https://youtu.be/4rvTppy1qLI
59. Schweifer, Johannes. *The Intrinsic Value of Bitcoin.* https://medium.com/@schweiferjohannes (2021).
60. Internet Protocol Suite. https://en.wikipedia.org/wiki/Internet_protocol_suite
61. Simple Mail Transfer Protocol. https://en.wikipedia.org/wiki/Simple_Mail_Transfer_Protocol
62. What is Bitcoin (BTC)? - First Blockchain and CryptoCurrency. https://atomicdex.io/en/blog/what-is-bitcoin-btc/
63. The Paypers. Argentine province Mendoza now accepts crypto for taxes and fees (August 2022).
64. Tuwiner, Jordan. Bitcoin Block Size Debate Wars Explained. Buy Bitcoin Worldwide (2023).
65. How does blockchain solve the Byzantine generals problem? Coin Telegraph.
66. Kaloudis, George. Celebrating Bitcoin Pizza Day. Coin Telegraph (May 22, 2023).
67. Srinivasan, Balaji. The Network State: How to Start a New Country (2022).
68. Casey and Vigna. The Truth Machine: The Blockchain and the Future of Everything. St.

Martin's Press (2018).

69. Weinberg, Joseph. Bitcoin enables sovereign individuality, our digital future's holy grail. Bitcoin Magazine (Nov. 25, 2021).
70. Wankum, Leon. Why Bitcoin is Digital Real Estate. Bitcoin Magazine (August 20, 2022).
71. Shark Tank Investor Kevin O'Leary Says He Considers Crypto a Stock Market Sector - Heres Why. *The Daily Hodl*. https://www.iqstock.news/n/shark-tank-investor-kevin-oleary-considers-crypto-stock-market-sector-heres-2822844/
72. https://fiatmarketcap.com, https://companiesmarketcap.com/assets-by-market-cap
73. https://explorer.btc.com/btc/transactionsThe privacy issues of central bank digital currencies (CBDCs): An overview
74. Emmanuel, Amosika. How Banks Try to Discredit Bitcoin. Bitcoin Magazine (May 6, 2022).
75. Panetta, Fabio. Paradise lost? How crypto failed to deliver on its promises and what to do about it. European Central Bank (June 2023).
76. Bindseil and Schaaf. Bitcoin's last stand. European Central Bank, blog post (November 30, 2022).
77. Lindrea, Brayden. Crypto is for criminals? JPMorgan has been fined $39B and has its own token. Coin Telegraph (December 5, 2023).
78. Braun, Helene. BlackRock, Valkyrie name authorized participants including JPMorgan for Bitcoin ETF. Coindesk (December 29, 2023).
79. Sergeenkov, Andrey. China Crypto Bans: A Complete History. Coindesk (May 11, 2023).
80. IMF urges El Salvador to remove Bitcoin as legal tender. BBC (January 26, 2022).
81. El Salvador angrily rejects IMF call to drop Bitcoin use. ApNews (January 31, 2022).
82. The First Gold Coin. *BullionByPost. https://www.bullionbypost.co.uk/index/gold/the-first-gold-coin/*
83. Bitcoin: The first digital monetary energy network, The Saylor Series Episode 4 (WiM004). https://youtu.be/1Ms7ql_S63A
84. Singh, Onkar. The privacy issues of central bank digital currencies (CBDCs): An overview. Coin Telegraph.
85. O'Neill Paese, Kathleen. FedNow: A Once-in-a-Generation Payments Innovation for the Fed. Federal Reserve Bank of St. Louis (September 6, 2023).
86. Quarmby, Brian. Presidential hopefuls RFK Jr. and Ron DeSantis rail against FedNow. Coin Telegraph (April 11, 2023).
87. Foss, Greg. Oil will soon be priced in Bitcoin as petrodollar collapses. Kitco News (May 30, 2023).
88. Fox Business Network interview with BlackRock CEO Larry Fink (July 5, 2023). https://youtu.be/cX4FvW_Ph_s
89. Bambrough, Billy. This Is Just The Beginning' —BlackRock CEO Reveals Massive Crypto Plan After ETF Sparks Wild Bitcoin And Ethereum Price Swings. Forbes (January 14, 2024).

90. Simply Bitcoin interview with Jurrien Timmer, Fidelity Investments (November 3, 2023). https://youtu.be/7gHDX0a317e.
91. David Lin Report. Billionaire Tim Draper on Bitcoin's Long-Term Value (October 28, 2023). https://youtu.be/iCH9R4wsZik
92. U.S. Consumer Debt Crisis. https://www.debt.org/faqs/americans-in-debt/
93. Hayek, Friedrich A. The Use of Knowledge in Society. American Economic Association (1945).
94. Why Do Starlings Flock in Murmurations? https://youtu.be/QvQZU6VAuao
95. Kucoin. Understanding Crypto Users in Turkey: More Than Half of Turkish Adults Invest in Crypto (August 31, 2023).
96. Griffin, G. Edward. The Creature from Jekyll Island: A Second Look at the Federal Reserve. Amer Media (1995).
97. Bitcoin Magazine. What happens after a bitcoin ETF is approved? Backstage with Dylan LeClair (September 2023).
98. Di Salvo, Mat. BlackRock CEO Larry Fink: Crypto Will 'Transcend Any One Currency'. Decrypt (July 14, 2023).
99. First Letter of St. Paul to Timothy, 1 Timothy 6:10. https://www.biblegateway.com/passage/?search=1+timothy+6%3A10&version=RSV
100. The Book of Exodus, 20:3. https://www.biblegateway.com/passage/?search=exodus+20%3A3&version=RSV
101. Gospel of Matthew, 19:23-24. https://www.biblegateway.com/passage/?search=matthew+19%3A23-24&version=RSV
102. Gospel of Matthew, 19:21-22. https://www.biblegateway.com/passage/?search=matthew+19%3A21-22&version=RSV
103. Gospel of Mark, 12:41-44. https://www.biblegateway.com/passage/?search=mark+12%3A41-44&version=RSV
104. The Book of Exodus, 20:15. https://www.biblegateway.com/passage/?search=exodus+20%3A15&version=RSV
105. Archana, Alekh. How Nirav Modi pulled off the great Indian bank robbery. Mint (February 2018).
106. Greenberg, Andy. Crypto is anything but private. https://time.com/6239364/crypto-criminals-andy-greenberg
107. World Population Review. Oil Reserves by Country.
108. Amadeo, Kimberly. Hyperinflation. Its Causes and Effects with Examples (July 2022).
109. Thomas, Jeff. Wheelbarrow Economics. https://internationalman.com/articles/wheelbarrow-economics/
110. 9 mind-blowing facts about Venezuela's economy. (2019). *Market Insider*. https://markets.businessinsider.com/news/stocks/venezuela-economy-facts-2019-5-1028225117

111 Quittem, Brandon. *Bitcoin is a Pioneer Species*. Robert Breedlove - The "What is Money?" Show, Episode 161 (2022).

112 Harding, Lee. Trucker convoy leader Chris Barbers continues to fight for freedom. Western Standard (June 11, 2023).

113 TD Bank freezes two personal accounts that received over $1M for trucker convoy. https://globalnews.ca/news/8615490/td-bank-freezes-accounts-trucker-convoy

114 Ventura, Luca. World's Most Unbanked Countries 2021. *Global Finance Magazine* (2021).

115 Buchwald, Elisabeth. Banks aren't out of the woods after the collapse of SVB and Signature. CNN (April 25, 2023).

116 U.S. Senator for North Carolina. Budd introduces bill to empower individuals to control their own digital assets. Press Release (November 7, 2023).

117 Harper, Colin. Multisignature Wallets Can Keep Your Coins Safer-If You Use Them Right. *Coindesk* (2020).

118 Rybarczyk, Armstrong and Fabiano. On *Bitcoin's Energy Consumption*. Galaxy Digital (2021).

119 Africans are pioneering the bright yet complicated green future of Bitcoin mining. Forbes.com (May 2023).

120 El Salvador partnership to build $1 billion bitcoin mining farm. Reuters (June 5, 2023).

121 Hobard, Mike. How Bitcoin Mining Strengthens Electricity Grids. Bitcoin Magazine (March 12, 2022).

122 Stossel TV - The Full Alex Epstein: The Moral Case for Fossil Fuels, Renewable Energy, and Green Deceptions (2023). https://youtu.be/R00TO3D3f5A

123 Pope Leo XIII, Rerum Novarum – Encyclical on Capital and Labor (1891).

124 Laudato Si', Encyclical Letter of Pope Francis on Care for our Common Home, Chapter 2, #26 and #27 (2016).

125 Franklin D. Roosevelt, 32nd President of the United States of America. The White House.

126 The S&P Sectors. https://corporatefinanceinstitute.com/resources/knowledge/finance/the-sp-sectors/

127 Shark Tank Investor Kevin OLeary Says He Considers Crypto a Stock Market Sector-Here's Why. (2021). *The Daily Hodl*.

128 Brett, Jason. Senators Reintroduce Landmark Crypto Bill Amid Heavy Competition And Regulatory Turf Battles. Forbes, July 13, 2023.

129 Galatians 5:1. https://www.biblegateway.com/passage/?search=Galatians%205%3A1&version=RSV

130 Book of Acts 9:1https://youtu.be/PhKXneIMA_47-18. https://www.biblegateway.com/passage/?search=acts+9%3A17-18&version=RSV

131 1 Corinthians 9:19. https://www.biblegateway.com/passage/?search=1+corinthians+9%3A19&version=RSV

132 Lankow, Jason. Hyperinflation: The Story of 9 Failed Currencies (2022).
133 Backhouse, Fid. et al. Hyperinflation in the Weimar Republic – German History. Britannica.com.
134 Trading Economics. Lebanon Inflation Rate (2022).
135 Mohal, Joshi. US Dollar Collapse Predictions: The Dollar is on its way out (2022).
136 Kelly, Jack. Sports stars and politicians are taking their pay in Bitcoin and other cryptocurrencies – would you? Forbes (2022).
137 Chainanalysis Team. The 2022 Global Crypto Adoption Index (September 2022).
138 Germo, Marvin. The Internet and Bitcoin: A Comparison of Adoption Rates and Potential for Mass Adoption. LinkedIn (January 29, 2023).
139 Peterson, Timothy F. Metcalfe's Law as a Model for Bitcoin's Value. Cane Island Alternative Investors (2018).
140 Cardinal Turkson. *Mensorum Bonam* – Faith-Based Measures for Catholic Investors: A Starting Point and Call to Action. The Pontifical Academy of Social Sciences (2022).
141 Why Capitalism is Good and We Don't Need Inflationary Money – The Principles of Economics with Saifedean. Coin Stories Podcast by Natalie Brunell (July 2023).
142 Archdiocese of Toronto, Sacrament of Reconciliation for Adults. https://www.archtoronto.org/siteassets/media/offices--ministries/sub-sites/day-of-confessions/guide-adult-en-2016.pdf
143 St. Paul's Letter to the Colossians 3:2.
144 Gospel of Matthew 6:19-21. https://www.biblegateway.com/passage/?search=matthew+6%3A19-21&version=RSV
145 Ammous, Saifedean. The Bitcoin Standard: The Decentralized Alternative to Central Banking. Wiley (2018).
Casey and Vigna. The Truth Machine: The Blockchain and the Future of Everything. Picador (2019).
Booth, Jeff. The Price of Tomorrow: Why Deflation is the Key to an Abundant Future. Stanley Press (2020).
Ammous, Saifedean. The Principles of Economics. The Saif House (2023).

Manufactured by Amazon.ca
Bolton, ON